Without imagination, nothing in the world could be meaningful. Without imagination, we could never make sense of our experience. Without imagination, we could never reason toward knowledge of reality.

MARK JOHNSON

Imagination is more important than knowledge. For knowledge is limited to all we now know and understand, while imagination embraces the entire world, and all there ever will be to know and understand.

ALBERT EINSTEIN

JOAN: *I hear voices telling me what to do. They come from God.*
BAUDRICOURT: *They come from your imagination.*
JOAN: *Of course. That is how the messages of God come to us.*

GEORGE BERNARD SHAW, *Saint Joan*

Imagination and the Journey of Faith

•   •

Sandra M. Levy

WILLIAM B. EERDMANS PUBLISHING COMPANY

GRAND RAPIDS, MICHIGAN / CAMBRIDGE, U.K.

Published 2008 by

Wm. B. Eerdmans Publishing Co.

2140 Oak Industrial Drive N.E., Grand Rapids, Michigan 49505 /

P.O. Box 163, Cambridge CB3 9PU U.K.

www.eerdmans.com

Printed in the United States of America

14 13 12 11 10 09 08   7 6 5 4 3 2 1

Library of Congress Cataloging-in-Publication Data

Levy, Sandra M.

Imagination and the journey of faith / Sandra M. Levy.

p.   cm.

Includes bibliographical references.

ISBN 978-0-8028-6301-0 (pbk.: alk. paper)

1. Imagination — Religious aspects — Christianity.

2. Faith.   I. Title.

BR115.I6L48   2008

233′.5 — dc22

2008015559

**The author and publisher gratefully acknowledge permission
to reprint the following materials:**

Excerpt from "Awaiting a Prayer" from *Love's Immensity: Mystics on the Endless Life* by Scott Cairns. Copyright © 2007 by Scott Cairns. Used by permission of Paraclete Press.

Excerpt from "The Empty Church" from *Frequencies* by R. S. Thomas. Copyright © 2001 by Kunjana Thomas and used by permission.

Excerpt from "In Whom We Live and Move and Have Our Being" from *Sands of the Well* by Denise Levertov. Copyright © 1997 by Denise Levertov. Reprinted by permission of New Directions Publishing Corp. and Pollinger limited.

"Hints and Glimpses" from *Hints and Glimpses* by Bonnie Thurston. Copyright © 2004 by Bonnie Thurston. Reprinted by permission of Three Peaks Press.

"Via Negativa" from *R. S. Thomas*. Copyright © 2001 by Kunjana Thomas and used by permission.

"We travelers" and "Up in the blown-down woods" from *Given* by Wendell Berry. Copyright © 2005 by Wendell Berry. Reprinted by permission of Shoemaker & Hoard Publishers.

*This book is dedicated
to the memory of my father,
who had a wonderful imagination,
and who told me stories that lit up my world.*

Contents

Preface

This book is rooted deeply in my life. The most proximate context was a richly rewarding sabbatical period I spent at Cambridge University in England, where, supported in part by a grant from the Lilly Foundation, I pursued an idea seeded in seminary years before. The question that drove me concerned the role that the human imagination plays in the development of religious faith. My curiosity about the imagination's role in religious belief was in part grounded in my training as a clinical psychologist in my early adult years. Although I am now an ordained clergy with theological training, my earlier shaping as a psychologist colored my understanding of the interplay between our behavior and our mental or cognitive power to make sense of the world around us.

So the intellectual roots for this project are embedded in two worlds of professional training — with some existential philosophy thrown in for good measure. But why does someone bother to write a book? After all, this present work was more than four years in the making, and it turned out to be a labor of love. Someone said in effect that you write a particular book because you have to. I believe that the emotion which feeds the drive to complete such a project is finally personal. So the deepest root of all that nourished me through this labor was a lifetime of personal experience with people near to me, some of whom I love, many of whom I care for in one way or another.

At the heart of my work, fueling my emotional commitment, lie two images. One is the image of so many I have met along the way who hunger for some sense of Transcendence in their lives. In one way or another, these individuals seem to possess imaginations that open out onto symbols and metaphors hinting of a transcendent Other whom some name God. The other image is of some individuals — several very dear to me — who seem to close off any imaginative engagement with such symbols of Transcendence.

My belief is that such glimmers of the sacred can be found in the everyday of ritual and metaphor, as well as in the rich store of creative symbolic expressions of Christian, Jewish, and Muslim traditions — poetry, song, art, story. Such creative products could act as conduits for transcendent experience if the human perceivers could only attune to them and engage them with their imaginations.

My original hunch, which has become strengthened through years of research and writing, is that our imaginative power, the creative imagination with which all humans are hardwired, lies at the heart of our potential encounter with some transcendent Reality. And my training as a psychologist has led me to think that if it is the case that all humans have the potential for such imaginative expression and engagement — that all are genetically given the power to create and imagine what is beyond the concrete given before them — then, like any other human faculty, the imagination can be enhanced by certain spiritual exercises and practices.

And so this book. In the first section I strive to make the case for the importance of the imagination in our meeting with God or Transcendence, and I address major categories of imaginative "products" — ritual, song, poetry, art, and story — through which Transcendence can be met. In the second section I turn to practices based on each of these categories, both in the home and community and in the worship place, exercises that can strengthen and enhance the imaginative capacity which each of us inherits by virtue of being human.

Because I believe so deeply in the importance of this topic in our postmodern, mostly secular, troubled world, with so many struggling for some meaning in their lives that runs deeper than our consumer culture, I have tried hard to make this book's content accessible to a wide readership. In addition to friends and former and current parishioners who have greatly encouraged me, I have had wonderful critical help as this project has been shaped over time.

First, I am deeply grateful to my long-suffering and very supportive husband and my two sons, who have patiently listened and read parts of the book along the way. My dear friends Anita and Anne did their part by reading each chapter in its first draft, pointing out things that baffled them in the early writing.

In addition, of course, my great thanks go to Jon Pott, the editor in chief at Eerdmans, for having faith in this project and faith in my ability to accomplish it. Without his suggestions, guidance, and support, this work would never have seen the light of day. I am also deeply grateful for the careful editing carried out by Mary Hietbrink, who saved me from several embarrassments along the way. She was a joy to work with in completing this book. Catherine Wallace, my friend and intellectual colleague, was also invaluable in reading the penultimate manuscript and giving her critical and intuitive input during the final stage of the project.

But my most profound gratitude and deepest thanks go to Professor Paul Achtemeier, close friend and dear colleague, who has acted as local editor, reading each chapter twice and the manuscript as a whole more than once. His critical comments and suggestions, along with his support and encouragement, have meant the world to me in the development of this work. This labor of love would have been much the poorer without his advice and critique.

Why Imagination Matters
in the Journey of Faith

[This search for Transcendence] may take many forms: an affir-
mation of faith, the gropings and glimpses of the sacred within
oneself, the aspirations for an ideal world beyond the self, vision-
ary glimpses of the sacred in another person or in the sublimity
of nature. But whatever form it takes, it is a search that is finally
beyond the power of words or of mere metaphor. Even [the imag-
ination's] symbol can never fully capture it, but it can begin to
express and embrace it.

J. Robert Barth, S.J.,
The Symbolic Imagination[1]

Whether or not you're a churchgoer, whether or not you've ever turned
a page of the Bible — if you've grown up in North American culture,
you most likely know the stories of the three wise men and the "shepherds keeping watch over their flocks by night." Many years ago, a wise
man I knew blended those two stories into a single story of his own
about religious faith. By describing the journey of the shepherds from
the field to the cave, their breathless and joyful running, their seemingly easy time of credulous belief, and contrasting that with the long,
slow, arduous, risky, perhaps question-filled journey of the wise seekers

---

1. J. Robert Barth, S.J., *The Symbolic Imagination* (New York: Fordham University
Press, 2001), pp. 143-44.

from the East, my friend spun a beautiful metaphor for different journeys of religious faith. One type of journey was not better than the other; both led to the divine infant at the end.

But the point which my friend emphasized and which has remained with me all these years is that those careful seekers, embarking on their slow, questioning, deliberative journey, were already caught up in a genuine faith quest from the first step of their venture. In some real sense they were already in a condition or state of faith, or they would not have bothered with the questions at all.

Now, when I look around me, the metaphor fits so many I know. In my life, both before and after my becoming an Episcopal priest, I have known many whose faith, either from cradle or from midlife "born-again" conversion, was seemingly without struggle, was apparently an easy journey of unquestioning belief. And I have known many others who question, who struggle with doubts of all kinds, who wonder about the existence of God, yet feel drawn — indeed, compelled — to ask the questions and to take the journey as best they can.

But here is my question. Why are there others who never bother to take the journey at all? Why are some seemingly impervious to the pull of these larger questions? Why are so many seemingly content to live out their lives within the everyday frames of family, market, and sport, without addressing larger questions of ultimate meaning?

This is not to say that there are not many good people within this latter category, some within my own family — good human beings who do the best they can to get along in our consumer-driven culture. Yet if you yourself start from the position that there is a level of meaning beyond your own concerns, that there is an Other beyond your own subjective projection, then it is clear that some may differ from you in their openness to that dimension of reality that transcends our particular material space. To return to the journey metaphor: Some travel hard, some travel easy, and some travel seemingly not at all to approach that Other beyond their own individual sphere of concern.

So then, why do some who perhaps ask questions of ultimate meaning but who do not see God, or a transcendent Other in any religious sense, as part of the equation — why do they not concern themselves with setting out on that faith journey? Why do they not appear to be open to questions of transcendent meaning or immortality or soul?

I believe that one answer to this question lies at the heart of this book. And that is the role of the *imagination,* the imaginative faculty, in opening up a meeting place between the transcendent Other and us. By *imagination* I do not mean what is commonly assumed by the term — that is, mere products of fancy without any status in reality (i.e., "It's only in your imagination, dear!"). Nor am I using the term in the limited sense of images, dreams, or "pictures" held in the mind. *What I mean by imagination here is the inherent human power to transcend the concrete, to create new images or ideas that can open up new possibility and promise — the not-yet of a future we can envision, the re-valuing of a remembered past. Ultimately what I mean by imagination is that human capacity to receive and respond to God's revelation in our everyday lives.* I believe that it is this human capacity which plays a key role in faith development.

Unfortunately, I think a strong case can be made that in general there has been a depletion or emptying out of the religious imagination in our modern/postmodern culture. Although both science and the marketplace within our democratic society have contributed a great deal to modern human welfare, we have paid a high cultural price in the process. Relationships have become a cost/benefit exchange, with the financial bottom line driving most decisions from prenuptial agreements to end-of-life arrangements. Charles Taylor[2] and others argue that such an outlook finally empties human life of its richness, its depth, and any sense of profound meaning.

One consequence of such emptying is a loss of vision and a loss of passion for life. Nothing is really worth dying for. Life has no deep purpose. Others have referred to the loss of "enchantment," the erosion of a sense of mystery or the sacred, where the world is simply made up of potential means to our own material ends. And as the individual has increasingly withdrawn into self-contained, technocratic, professional groupings or isolated units, the richness of community life has been all but lost.

Douglas Coupland is a Canadian writer who emerged on the literary scene in 1991 with his *Generation X: Tales for an Accelerated Culture.*[3] Other books of his followed, including *Life after God* in 1995, an account

2. Charles Taylor, *Sources of the Self: The Making of the Modern Identity* (Cambridge: Harvard University Press, 1989).

3. Douglas Coupland, *Generation X: Tales for an Accelerated Culture* (New York: St. Martin's Press, 1991).

of spiritual yearning in a postreligious age. In an article published by the *Christian Century* in 2000, he is quoted commenting on the development of his literary characters. He notes that not one of them has any kind of religious upbringing. As one says in *Life after God,* "You are the first generation raised without God."[4]

In that same article, Coupland points out that lack of religious upbringing is not the same as atheism. He says that the latter is not new. "That's been going on for thousands of years. What is new is that for the first time you had parents in the '50s, '60s, and '70s who found it was liberating to raise kids without any religion. If you didn't have those Easter egg hunts or pictures of Jesus when you grew up . . . you have nothing. *Ex nihilo.*" Describing himself as growing up in a "completely secular household" in a "completely secular neighborhood," he observes that "that germ of Judeo-Christian thinking wasn't there to begin with. You can't imagine it there. It simply wasn't there. [Don't presume] that I'm some lapsed Christian. I'm not. I'm working from zero."[5]

Still, in his characters and in his life, Coupland expresses a longing for deeper, religious meaning. Like the magi, he seems to be on a quest for a coherent sense of reality that includes a transcendent Other as ultimate horizon. And this quest seems to be shared by many others in our essentially secular society who may also be starting from near zero.

I think there is a sense of "Something there," even if it remains undefined. In fact, polls show that 75 percent of Americans believe in the existence of heaven and hell; and probably 90 percent of Americans believe in God — undefined but sensed. This persistent reach for "Something there" shows itself everywhere in our popular culture. Ghosts and goblins, angels and aliens, superstitions and spirit guides, crystals and channels, ESP and the occult — interest in all these things abounds. Those who are spiritually hungry mix and match a little of this and a little of that, borrowing from Zen or the Native American spirit world, weaving the whole into some kind of patchwork spiritual embrace.

Clearly the power of the imagination is richly displayed in creative constructions of a religious reality ranging from the do-it-yourself eso-

---

4. Douglas Coupland, *Life after God* (New York: Simon & Schuster/Pocket Books, 1994).

5. Cited in J. Brent Brill's article "Loneliness Virus: Douglas Coupland's World," *Christian Century,* 8 November 2000, p. 1152.

teric to the downright bizarre. But I believe that this creative power also lies at the heart of *all* religious experience, from Orthodox Judeo-Christianity to Islam to Zen to the occult. Our imagination does lie at the heart of our meeting with this Something or Someone, this Other which various faith communities name God.

Bonnie Thurston expresses this intuitive sense of Other in poetic form:

> All we have
> are hints and glimpses,
> something seen fleetingly
> as in peripheral vision,
> a shadowy shape
> beyond the drape,
> the voice that whispers
> behind the grill,
> the merest murmur
> of Elysian melody,
> a prickling of the skin
> which might be
> but a draft
> from an open window.
> But it is the window
> opening on eternity,
> seen now darkly,
> but then
> face to face.[6]

And it is out of this experience, this intuition of the Other's presence however named, that our imagination — in Thurston's words, that "window opening on eternity" — creates meaning. And what the imagination makes of this experience is shaped by our culture, our language, our personal experience, and our conversations with significant others around us.

For example, if I turn first to my own experience during private prayer, when I'm not tired or distracted by my overburdened to-do list,

6. Bonnie Thurston, "Hints and Glimpses," in *Hints and Glimpses* (Abergavenny, Great Britain: Three Peaks Press, 2004), p. 8.

when I quiet down and am very still, then I do have a strong sense of an Other, an intuited Presence within and around me. And since I was raised a Christian and am now an ordained clergy and an associate of a monastic order, it's hard for me to disentangle my sense of an Other from my images of Christ that I carry around in my head, from fleeting pictures of Jesus painted in the various Gospel stories. But still, underneath all of these images there is a sense of Other, a divine Presence in and around me that I believe is prior to and more fundamental than the Christian symbols that my imagination gives rise to.

William James, in his *Varieties of Religious Experience,*[7] includes the following case example:

> Quite early in the night I was awakened. . . . I felt as if I had been aroused intentionally, and at first thought some one was breaking into the house. . . . I then turned on my side to go to sleep again, and immediately felt a consciousness of a presence in the room . . . not the consciousness of a live person, but of a spiritual presence. . . . *I felt also at the same time a strong feeling of superstitious dread, as if something strange and fearful were about to happen.*[8]

Like this individual, not only do I experience, but I experience *something,* and it's that *something* that gets "fit into" my ongoing life story, that gets imagined symbolically and given a name. But again, the basic perceptual given that we make something of is an intuited Something or Someone that impinges. And again I, along with others, would maintain that it is that Other that is given to our awareness which is at least sometimes validly called God.[9]

---

7. William James, *Varieties of Religious Experience,* centenary edition (New York: Routledge, 2002). In 1901 and 1902, James delivered the Gifford Lectures at the University of Edinburgh to promote along with others the study of natural theology in a world increasingly shaped by enlightened science. His twenty lectures were published under this title, and became one of the most influential treatments of religious experience in America.

8. James, *Varieties of Religious Experience,* p. 53, emphasis added.

9. Of course, just because something is *named* as God, such a self-report is not necessarily true. The mystics down through the ages have been well aware that the devil is a trickster, and numerous tests have been devised that challenge the authenticity of such reports of divine experience. We'll return to this issue later in this work, but James, as well as other philosophers and theologians, have generally wound up pointing to the "fruits" of religious experience as the ultimate hallmark of their genuine character. "By

As an example of such an encounter with an Other with life-changing consequence, James reports the case of M. Alphonse Ratisbonne, ethnically a Jew but otherwise a secular, nonobservant Jew, who suddenly converted to Catholicism in Rome in 1842. In a subsequent letter to a friend, Ratisbonne described his experience:

> . . . You may ask me how I came to this new insight, for truly I had never opened a book of religion nor even read a single page of the bible. . . . But how came I, then, to this perception of it? I can answer nothing save this, that on entering that church I was in darkness altogether, and on coming out of it I saw the fullness of the light. I can explain the change no better than by the simile of a profound sleep or the analogy of one born blind who should suddenly open his eyes to the day. . . . *Without having any knowledge of the letter of religious doctrine, I now intuitively perceived its sense and spirit. Better than if I saw them, I felt those hidden things, I felt them by the inexplicable effects they produced in me.* It all happened in my interior mind; and those impressions, more rapid than thought, shook my soul, revolved and turned it, as it were, in another direction, towards other aims, by other paths.[10]

Here seems to be a case of some objective incursion into consciousness of an Other or Something that shook this man to the core, transforming his vision and his life. And it seems to be the case that he certainly did not have a Christian belief system or much if any knowledge of traditional Scripture or theology to "set him up" to imagine or make something religious out of his experience. But Ratisbonne had grown up in a western European culture, and at that moment he was physically in a small church, surrounded by religious symbols. Thus, his imaginative power wove together images and their meaning given and shaped by his culture, creating a meaning for him based on the experience — the Divine that broke through to his awareness on that day.

These examples prompt questions. How exactly does the imagination work? And what actual role does it play in the faith journey? Why are some individuals more open to novel input, ready to explore the unexpected that darts in from outside or at the margins of awareness,

---

their fruits ye shall know them." Ultimately, genuine religious experience should shape and transform an individual's behavior in the direction of virtue.

10. James, *Varieties of Religious Experience,* pp. 176-78, emphasis added.

more imaginatively open to such impingement? If we can address these questions here, then we may discover ways to enhance this human capacity to receive and creatively respond to God's revelation in our everyday lives, deepening our faith in the process.

In this introduction as well as in later chapters, I have drawn upon the work of Samuel Taylor Coleridge, a major poet, critic, and philosopher of the nineteenth-century Romantic period. In his *Biographia Literaria,*[11] Coleridge explicitly links the symbolic imagination with our direct experience of God — in fact, he identifies it as the primary access to God. Thus, Coleridge's writings and, indeed, his spirit hover over this entire volume, and the discerning reader will hear his thoughts as we turn to our topic at hand.

Coleridge and his friend William Wordsworth, as well as other English writers of the late eighteenth and early nineteenth century, were part of a romantic literary and artistic movement that caught fire not only in England but also in France, Germany, and America. This movement was in part a reaction to the rationalism of the Enlightenment, and so it celebrated the expression of emotion in art forms, particularly poetry. The imagination was of central interest as a human faculty reflecting creative freedom of spirit, and nature itself was seen as encompassing or incarnating a transcendent Spirit to be discovered and revered.

Coleridge had an extraordinary intellect, and his writings ranged from such poetic forms as *The Rime of the Ancient Mariner* and *Christabel,* to literary and political critiques, to theological treatises. In his personal life he was haunted by lost loves and by a chronic addiction to opium, and his remarkable productivity despite such episodic torment is testament to his genius.

Shortly after Coleridge's death, Charles Lamb, his good and nearly lifelong friend, wrote, "His great and dear Spirit haunts me. I cannot think a thought, I cannot make a criticism of men and books, without . . . reference to him. He was the proof and touchstone of all my cogitations. . . . Never saw I his likeness, nor probably can the world see it again."[12]

11. Samuel Taylor Coleridge, *Biographia Literaria, or Biographical Sketches of My Literary Life and Opinions,* ed. James Engell and W. Jackson Bate (Princeton: Princeton University Press, 1983).

12. Quoted in Richard Holmes, *Coleridge: Darker Reflections, 1804-1834* (New York: Pantheon Books, 1998).

And so Coleridge also haunts this present volume. Let's look first at his understanding of the imagination and its function as a conduit of the Divine.

The Primary and the Secondary Imagination

Coleridge divides the concept of the imagination into what he refers to as the primary and the secondary imagination.[13] What Coleridge means by the primary imagination is our basic mental capacity to see and organize stimuli from the world around us. As he defines it, this organizing capacity has creative, synthesizing, and unifying power that is God-given — in fact, it is a fundamental, creative power that we share with the Divine. In exercising its creative function, we act in the image of God.[14]

Coleridge thus sees this power of the primary imagination as incarnated in human beings and, as such, as part of our essential equipment. Humans participate in and re-enact God's creative Being through the power of their imagination. The mind's power to order the reality around it is a God-given and grace-filled one that all humans possess and express more or less adequately in their lives.

Coleridge uses the term "secondary imagination" to refer to the human ability to transcend this primary organization, to reassemble perceptual elements or fragments and create *new* meaning, ultimately grasping for fuller and deeper meaning in our search for union with the Divine.

The point here is that, for Coleridge, this primary and secondary

13. Apparently, Coleridge "borrowed" liberally from the writings of a German psychologist, Johan Tetens, who had already characterized the workings of the primary and the secondary imagination in a two-volume work published in Leipzig in 1777. Thomas McFarland, in his *Originality and Imagination* (Baltimore: Johns Hopkins University Press, 1985), concludes that "the lineage of the secondary imagination extends not only backward beyond Kant to Tetens, but also beyond Tetens to Leibniz, and finally beyond Leibniz to Plato. With antecedents of this kind, it is inevitable that Coleridge's . . . theory of the imagination actually bears less on poetry than it does on those things that always mattered most to him . . . [They are] the freedom of the will, the immortality of the soul, and the existence of God" (p. 118).

14. Coleridge says, "The primary IMAGINATION I hold to be the living Power and prime Agent of all human Perception, and as a repetition in the finite mind of the ethereal act of creation in the infinite I AM" (*Biographia Literaria,* vol. 1, chapter 13, p. 304).

imaginative power is a divinely given power that provides a direct conduit between the perceiving, creative human being and a Divine Being active in creation. As Robert Barth puts it so well, "The very act of imagination, then, whether of the secondary imagination in the creation of a symbol or of the primary imagination by which we perceive symbols [of God, the symbol-Giver, all around us], is for Coleridge itself a religious act — both in its origin, since it is empowered by God, and in its effect, since it allows us to perceive the eternal revealed in and through the temporal reality."[15] As Barth points out, the Transcendent (the eternal) and the world around us (the temporal) are mutually "translucent" to each other, since the same divine light shines through both.

The main point that I want to make is this: For Coleridge, our primary power to perceive symbols gleaned from the world about us (these pregnant signs of God's impinging presence and erupting action, generated by God and given for our reception), along with our secondary power to create new meaning through symbols (expressed in different ways through ritual, music, poetry, art, and story), is our opening onto the transcendent realm. The imagination thus becomes our gateway to God.

The Truth Value of Language

There is one further aspect of Coleridge's thought that I want to emphasize here. In *The Symbolic Imagination,* Robert Barth speaks of Coleridge's "fiduciary" view of language.[16] That is, in contrast to our own skeptical and sometimes cynical age that questions the possibility of knowing anything for sure, the tradition to which Coleridge belonged had absolute trust in the *possibility* of language to uncover and express the deepest truth about reality. And Coleridge believed that the highest possible expression of such language was in the form of metaphor and symbol, especially symbols found in poetic expression.

If you were to adopt such a view, you would take on trust — on faith, if you will — that metaphoric expressions, that symbolic forms

---

15. J. Robert Barth, *Romanticism and Transcendence* (Columbia: University of Missouri Press, 2003), p. 124.

16. Barth, *The Symbolic Imagination,* pp. 44-45.

can open us up to what is real. You would trust that at the edge of language, metaphoric symbols push back the borders of the unknown and open us out onto truth as we can grasp it. As Barth explains it, "Symbolic utterance, whether in words or gestures or images, can 'find' us, as Coleridge would say, and evoke a response of our whole being, leading us to even deeper perception of the reality opened up to us, both within and without."[17]

Thus, the imagination's symbol-making power allows us to deal with the paradoxes and contradictions that surround us, helping us to grasp a deeper truth beneath them. We can glimpse that beneath the horror of pain and death lies the promise of abundant life; that beyond doubt and anguish can lie faith nevertheless; that beneath the bite of satire lies a larger truth to tell. The work of the imagination in responding to and creating symbols in all their forms, from embodied symbols of ritual to metaphoric symbols of story, helps you and me cope with the contradictions and challenges of our finite human lives.

We live out our lives in time, moving from birth to death within a particular slice of history. Our very consciousness has a temporal shape to it, with the experience of our present moment including our past memories and our future hopes. We typically make sense out of our experience by imaginatively fitting it into a narrative — a "first this and then that" — using the language and symbols of our culture to tell our story. Thus we live out the story of our lives.

And as long as we are alive, our imaginations can create new meaning and can reshape the story by reconfiguring elements of our previous experience into new patterns. The earlier story of Ratisbonne provides an example. His report is that of a former unbeliever, someone who was caught off-guard and surprised by such unexpected impingement. Before his conversion, he presumably lacked any conscious religious belief. But apparently the gate of his imagination was open sufficiently to allow the symbolic repatterning of his life's meaning based on his encounter with the Other in that Roman church on that day. By means of such symbols and metaphors, he rewrote his life story, giving it a whole new meaning.

To sum up: Coleridge believed that it is through the primary and the secondary imagination, through the imaginative power to partici-

---

17. Barth, *The Symbolic Imagination,* p. 45.

pate in and create meaning, that we are open to truth through symbolic expression, meeting God in the process. God reaches out to us, and we reach out to God, "encountering each other in the joy of the symbolic act."[18]

For Coleridge, the imaginative expression of symbol is the reach, the struggle to articulate what has already truly been grasped as an encounter — in Barth's expression, "grasped without words — what has been felt in the bones, what has been dreamt, what has been glimpsed in vision. What is felt, what is known in the bones is the presence of this Other. The struggle to say is to express the truth of an encounter with the sacred, which has already occurred, and yet still takes place in and around the symbol."[19] Perhaps if we reflect on our own deepest instincts from time to time, we might also admit such a feeling in the bones, such hints and glimpses of some Other on the horizon of our consciousness.

The Imagination at Work

As we have seen, our imagination responds to and creates meaning through various symbolic expressions. Through symbols we encounter Transcendence; we glimpse truth beneath our everyday reality. But the meaning we attach to symbols is also shaped by our life experiences, so that meaning is open to growth and change. Thus, symbols and metaphors that we inherit from our cultural tradition not only have a historical significance but also take on new meaning arising from our present context. As Barth puts it, symbols remain open to "new uses in fresh and changing future contexts."[20] In other words, the imagination has a developmental aspect.

An illuminating example is provided by the autobiography of Reynolds Price, a writer and professor at Duke University. Price describes his struggle with terrible physical pain and paralysis that developed from a malignant spinal tumor. Early on in his treatment, he experienced some kind of mystical encounter with Transcendence. He

18. Barth, *The Symbolic Imagination,* p. 46.
19. Barth, *The Symbolic Imagination,* pp. 144-45.
20. Barth, *Romanticism and Transcendence,* p. 125.

reports having either a dream or a vision of Jesus leading him into the Sea of Galilee and washing him with handfuls of water while promising healing of his disease:

> Jesus silently took up handfuls of water and poured them over my head and back till water ran down my puckered scar. Then he spoke once — "Your sins are forgiven" — and turned to shore again, done with me.
>
> I came on behind him, thinking in standard greedy fashion, It's not my sins I'm worried about. So to Jesus' receding back, I had the gall to say, "Am I also cured?"
>
> He turned to face me, no sign of a smile, and finally said two words —
>
> "That too." Then he climbed from the water, not looking round, really done with me.[21]

Sometime later, Price confided to a friend what had happened to him. His friend asked him to draw what he'd seen — Jesus cupping the water over his head. And so he did. He sketched the two of them as they had stood in the water, the liquid flowing over the purple scar on Price's back. Price writes,

> The fact of regaining just that much on paper triggered the subject of all the dozens of drawings I'd make in the next two years. They were all, every one, meditations on the face of Jesus; and looking back through them now, I can wonder how I narrowed so much of my limited strength and hope for survival down to the space of a sheet of paper with a few brushed lines in search of the face that had driven Western art for more than a thousand years.[22]

Interestingly, Price notes that he was not a particularly religious person in any orthodox sense, but he had grown up in a Christian culture, surrounded by Christian symbols and stories. Here his imagination retrieves from memory a symbol from that tradition — the symbol of baptismal water — and he creates for himself, out of the pressure of his own life context, some vision of hope and healing.

---

21. Reynolds Price, *A Whole New Life* (New York: Penguin Books, 1995), p. 43.
22. Price, *A Whole New Life,* p. 75.

To sum up: Price's memory contained a rich store of images and symbols and meaningful metaphors that his imagination seized and wove into a whole episode rich with astonishingly new and deep meaning for him. In his dream or mystical vision (he couldn't identify the exact nature of this vivid, life-changing experience), his imagination opened him up to an encounter with what he believed was a figure of divine Transcendence. This encounter — through the symbol of water, which connoted for him cleansing and healing and new life — gave rise to a strong emotional response, a sense of joy and peace and well-being.

Although Christians usually take the symbol of water in baptism to mean rebirth, Price took it to indicate physical and emotional healing as well, a hope-filled cure from his disease. This development of the symbol's meaning beyond its traditional contours in the face of his own life context enabled Price to see some deeper meaning beneath his pain and suffering, reconciling his longing for wholeness with the obvious limits of his disease. This creative reconfiguring of the pattern of meaning in his life in response to the water/baptismal symbol also enabled him to cope better with his life-threatening struggles and gave him deep hope for his future well-being.

As we saw in Price's recounting of his experience, symbols, given by the imagination in the depths of memory, often reside below the surface of consciousness. T. S. Eliot asks, "Why, for all of us, out of all that we have heard, seen, felt, in a lifetime, do certain images recur, charged with emotion, rather than others?"[23] Such memories have symbolic value, but of what we cannot always completely grasp or put into words. But as Price's vision indicates, such symbols become a powerful means of creating and carrying meaning in our lives, giving us hope for our future.

For Coleridge and others, the imaginative capacity that lies at the heart of all such encounters with the Divine, this basic capacity for perceiving and ordering meaning out of perceptual chaos, is at least implicitly an act of faith, a fundamental trust that something true can emerge from our imaginative vision.

Can we then consider the personal breaking-in of the Transcendent in our everyday life a kind of revelation? In his discussion of belief sources, Robert Alston, like Coleridge, makes a strong case for the con-

---

23. T. S. Eliot, *The Use of Poetry and the Use of Criticism* (Cambridge: Harvard University Press, 1933), p. 148.

tral importance of *actually experiencing God's presence* as a primary source of belief.[24] The firsthand experience of the Divine explored here, that perceptual and imaginative openness to divine encounter which Price described, is in fact our primary access to perceiving God's actions and purposes for our everyday lives. Such openness to God's presence ultimately provides assurance that the Creator of the universe that revelation testifies to, that "Designer" that natural theology points to, that Prime Actor in the salvation drama that Scripture attests to — that this Being actually does exist.

Thus, our personal experience of God, and the perceptual attunement upon which such an encounter rests, remain central aspects of a personal belief structure. *At the heart of belief lies the capacity that our imagination affords to perceive God and to create the core meaning that can transform our lives.*

In his concluding remarks in his *Varieties of Religious Experience,* William James says, "I only translate into schematic language what I may call the instinctive belief of mankind: *God is real since he produces real effects. . . . We and God have business with each other; and in opening ourselves to his influence our deepest destiny is fulfilled.*"[25] And it is this "business" that we have with God, mediated by our perception and creatively filtered through our imagination, that lies at the core of religious belief. And that is, after all, the subject of this book.

The Imaginative Journey before Us

> . . . we ought
> first to keep an attentive mind, leaning in
> expectantly, and waiting on the God
> until He comes visiting the soul, making
> mysterious entry via any manner of
> countless paths — the openings
> and varied senses of the soul. . . .[26]

---

24. William P. Alston, *Perceiving God* (Ithaca, N.Y.: Cornell University Press, 1991).

25. James, *Varieties of Religious Experience,* pp. 398-99, emphasis added.

26. Scott Cairns, "Awaiting a Prayer" (lines 7-12), in *Love's Immensity: Mystics on the Endless Life* (Brewster, Mass.: Paraclete Press, 2007), p. 28.

As this excerpt from one of Scott Cairns's poems suggests, the imagination is our gateway to God. And like many gates, this one swings both ways. That is, through our God-given capacity to read symbols carrying glints of transcendent truth, we glimpse traces of the God who comes to us; through our imaginative powers, we create and co-create with others, through symbols (gesture, metaphor, sound, image, story), new worlds of meaning, running to meet God in the process. And each of these symbolic means opens up, in a unique way, different gateways to the Divine.

We get a different "slant" on the Divine, a different sort of glimpse of God through listening to music — the transport of a Bach cantata, for example — than through viewing Picasso's *Guernica*. We get a whole different sense of Transcendence reading the last page of a short story by Flannery O'Connor than that which we experience physically as we prostrate ourselves in ritual prayer. These various symbolic openings onto Transcendence — these "openings/and varied senses of the soul," as Cairns puts it — are not redundant categories of experience, substitutable for one another. Each form of symbolic expression "finds us" (as Coleridge would say) in a different way, refracting a different aspect of God's mystery, all of them together affording a deeper, richer experience of the Divine.

And so, in the three chapters that make up Section I, I will examine in turn each of these major modes of imaginative creation, each affording another way through our imagination's gateway to God. In Chapters One through Three I will explore the various ways in which humans encounter God and create symbolic meaning in their lives — specifically, through ritual and music (Chapter One), sacred and secular poetry and visual art (Chapter Two), and story as it is found in plays, films, novels, and Scripture (Chapter Three).

Section I will be followed by a coda, where I'll discuss the problem of truth criteria applied to the products of our imagination. How do we know whether what we have imagined has any validity? Since we are capable of generating both good and evil imaginings, what criteria do we apply to them in order to judge their worth? Given the basic assumption held here regarding the reality of a transcendent Other, how do we judge — within that framework — the goodness or validity of what our imagination produces?

And of course, like any other gate, our imaginative opening can swing wide open or can remain pushed closed and if not locked, at least ignored as a way out of our closed, mundane life. The imaginative power that we all possess by virtue of being human is shaped by our life experience, is thus vital or dormant, is open or relatively closed to new experience as a function of our personal backgrounds.

In Section II I will consider ways of enhancing this imaginative faculty through various practices. That is, once I've made the case that the imagination plays a key role in faith development, then I'll show how certain practices can enrich it. Here I will return to the questions I raised earlier: Why do some seemingly remain impervious to God's impingement? Why are some not attuned to God's grace-filled revelation? Why do some not bother to take that faith journey at all? If the answer partly lies in the exercise of the imagination or the lack thereof, then we must ask what can be done to open up that imaginative space in order to enhance the growth of faith in, say, a young adult who may hunger for something more in her life than "reality" TV shows, or the teen who may at some level hope for meaning beyond the drug culture, or the world of computer games?

For this reason, after I briefly take a closer look at the nature of the imagination itself in the Introduction to Section II, in Chapters Four and Five I will discuss spiritual practices both in the home and in communities and churches, covering the gamut of the imagination's symbolic expressions considered in this volume. These practices are aimed at strengthening the imaginative capacities of both youth and adults, involving ritual, poetry, storytelling, and the fine arts.

In Chapter Six, the final chapter, I will explore the overall implications of this work and the issues it raises, which I believe are deadly serious. Although writers in every age have raised the alarm about lost traditions and the danger for future generations, it seems to me that our particular historical situation is fraught with a new threat of spiraling meaninglessness among large segments of the population.

As Rowan Williams eloquently explains in his *Lost Icons,* our social meaning has been sucked into the vortex of the market, with all — including our children — becoming commodified in the process:

Individually, we find the possibilities of creative exchange and civility, beyond suspicion or rivalry, slipping away from us: there are fewer and fewer conversational others, because of the dominant myths of the authentic hidden self and of the all-pervasiveness of private and competitive interest. But if there were an "other" for humanity itself, an other innocent of human history and therefore outside the human economy of violence, wouldn't we be able to feel assured that we were, after all, the object of a benign gaze, that we were heard and seen as we needed to be?[27]

It is my hope and my goal in writing this book that possibilities can be opened up for faith development in those whose underdeveloped capacity for religious imagination may be inextricably linked with what Williams calls the "loss of what is encoded in the . . . icons of [a religious] tradition . . . the other who does not compete, with whom I don't have to and can't bargain; the other beyond violence."[28] As Williams observes, we can choose death, but we don't have to. I offer readers this book in hopes of life instead.

27. Rowan Williams, *Lost Icons: Reflections on Cultural Bereavement* (London: T&T Clark, 2003), pp. 207-8.
28. Williams, *Lost Icons*, p. 228.

SECTION I

CHAPTER ONE

Meeting God in Ritual

All those rituals trying to ease a departure:
Opening windows, wakes, keenings, devout
Observance of old ways that seemed to reassure
The living, to appease a spirit traveling out.
The same crying need for patterns, some way
To cope with our bafflement, just the relief
Of routines, customs, things to do or say,
Fragile ceremonies shaping a space for grief.

Michael O'Siadhail, "Three Wishes"[1]

It was the night of 9/11 at St. Mark's Church. Initially, we thought we'd hold a service of prayer and remembrance on the next night, when we had had more time to think through and organize the liturgy and music. I'd have time to pull my thoughts together and think about what I could possibly say to those gathered, what I would say about the meaning of the terrible thing that had happened to our country, to our community, to our souls.

But as the morning hours spilled into the afternoon of that day, somehow it became clear that we had to open our doors to the congre-

---

1. Michael O'Siadhail, "Three Wishes" (stanza 2, lines 1-8), found in his collected poems, *Our Double Time* (Trowbridge, Wiltshire, England: Cromwell Press Ltd., 1998), p. 47.

gation and to the community at large that same night. We realized that this couldn't wait until tomorrow.

So, thanks to the Internet and the phone, the doors were open by six P.M. on that fateful day. A large collection of bewildered and anxious human beings poured through those doors and gathered in the darkening church — to pray, to sing songs of lament, to hug and cry, to comfort, to look to someone to say something that would make sense out of what had happened. They came because human beings do seem to have a deep-rooted longing for ritual, for expressing through bodily movement, gesture, and words some profound sense of meaning that our world holds for us, to express symbolically some sense of our grasp of reality, of the world we inhabit. And as I climbed into the pulpit, I hoped and prayed that I could say something that would offer some modicum of hope and solace on that night.

Later, as we gathered around the communion table to share in the Eucharist, the bonds of community that bound us to one another and to all of suffering humanity were affirmed. The ancient words of the liturgy reminded every one of us that goodness and truth are stronger than evil. We also affirmed our hope in some deeper Reality beneath the horrors of the day that would sustain our country and, beyond that, would sustain humanity in all its travails. We knew at some basic, core level that out of the ashes of the World Trade Center would rise some deeper sense of goodness and purpose at the heart of it all.

Such was our hope, which seemed genuinely renewed in that ritual experience carried out by the gathered community on the night of the day that our country, as someone said, lost its innocence. Reflecting back on that night as I write this, I realize that it was not only a time of profound anguish and anxiety, but a time of searching and questioning, a time in which many displayed generosity and selfless sacrifice, a time of courage, of fortitude shown by many of our citizens, a fortitude that few knew was actually there before crisis revealed it.

Émile Durkheim, the nineteenth-century social philosopher, in his *Elementary Forms of Religious Life,*[2] said that a shared, communal misfortune enlivens a sense of human bonding. A death in the family or a

---

2. Émile Durkheim, *The Elementary Forms of Religious Life,* trans. Karen E. Fields (New York: Free Press, 1995); originally published as *Les Formes elementaires de la vie religieuse: Le systeme totemique en Australie* (Paris: Alcan, 1912).

death in a parish or a civic community group does seem to call forth the obligation to show up and share as members of that community the loss of one who belonged to it. And certainly the death of nearly three thousand of our compatriots seemed to arouse a societal need to mourn. In fact, according to Durkheim, one becomes morally bound to grieve, because not mourning somehow cuts one off from the bonds of that larger group.

Humans, like animals, seem in fact to be hardwired to perform ritual behaviors. Your dog circles around and around before finally lying down for that nap (considered innate, ritualized behavior by those who study such things); certain birds perform very elaborate mating rituals. Similarly, humans engage in mostly learned ritual behaviors, individually and idiosyncratically (e.g., always placing the toothbrush to the right of the drinking cup and always, always sleeping on the left side of the bed), as well as corporately (e.g., the ritual of watching Monday-night football in season, the ritual of pledging allegiance before the local baseball game can begin). In fact, we engage in multiple rituals every day.

In *Metaphors We Live By*,[3] authors George Lakoff and Mark Johnson view both personal and shared rituals as embodied symbolic practices that help give coherence, structure, and significance to our actions, thus reducing randomness and chaos in our everyday lives. From our everyday rituals, such as always watching CNN News before bedtime or always taking a multivitamin before breakfast, to the most solemn religious rite, such as the Eucharist celebration on Sunday or the once-a-year Seder meal, all are "repeated structured practices," some consciously and culturally designed, others arising spontaneously in everyday life.[4]

The communal gathering at St. Mark's on the night of 9/11 serves as an example of the interweaving of ritual and story. It involved both ritualistic, bodily expression — gestures of comfort, postures of prayer, my climb to the pulpit to convey words of solace, the reception of bread and wine at the communion table — and ancient story preached and

3. George Lakoff and Mark Johnson, *Metaphors We Live By* (Chicago: University of Chicago Press, 1980).

4. In fact, everyday rituals are very revealing because usually they reflect our values and our sense of self in the world. As these authors point out, the values we live by are probably reflected most strongly in these little things we do repeatedly.

embedded in liturgical texts and hymns that filled out and conveyed the meaning of our gathering. This is a point I will stress in this chapter and beyond: that bodily ritual and story are intertwined. Our imaginations blend symbols expressed in gesture with metaphoric myths and sacred stories to create meaning at all levels of our experience.

Embodied Meaning and Ritual Knowledge

Before analyzing the imagination's work through bodily experience, I want to offer a taste of individual ritual practice by relating two different stories.

The first story is mine. In the late 1980s, my husband and I attended a conference in Jerusalem. While there, we walked the cobblestone streets of the old walled city, tracing with others the traditional footsteps of Jesus as he struggled to make his way to Golgotha and his crucifixion, outside the gates of the old city. As any of you know who have stepped inside a Roman Catholic or Anglo-Catholic church, there are traditionally fourteen "stations" or stops along the way, representing events that, according to tradition, occurred on the Via Dolorosa, that last walk before Jesus' death (for example, Jesus' falling three times under the weight of the cross and his encountering the women of Jerusalem who were lamenting for him). Despite the somewhat touristy flavor of that Jerusalem walk, it was memorable. In fact, about halfway through the tour, it became quite moving. I could imagine Jesus' feet touching the very same cobblestones that my feet were touching at that moment. I experienced almost a sense of being there, of being part of that crowd, of witnessing Jesus' struggle and suffering. It became a surprisingly profound experience that remains vivid in my imagination to this day.

The second story comes from writer and theologian Tom Driver, who relates an experience he had after returning from a trip to India:

> Standing at the kitchen stove early in the morning, looking past it through an open window, I feel sleepy . . . waiting for the coffee water to boil. An impulse to pray arises in me, but the thought of God remains as vague and unfocused as I feel myself to be. . . . I am not in the mood for words. . . . Without consciously thinking what to do, I

find myself raising my hands in front of my face and putting palms together, the way Indians do in their gesture of respect. Quickly, my emotions change. I become aware of a stir of energy throughout my body. My hands, palms still together, move downward until they are in front of my navel. I feel centered for the first time since arising. . . . During this little rite . . . no words pass through my consciousness. . . . It was a short and subtle ritual of transformation.[5]

These two examples of individual ritual practice show the imagination at work. Drawing on a rich store of cultural symbols that conveyed powerful, transcendent meaning, the ritual actions of path-following on pilgrimage and hand-gesturing in silent, wordless prayer had an emotional impact akin to awe. For both Driver and me, these ritual actions seemed to open up an encounter with the Other. Our experience of the moment was transformed into one fraught with religious significance — a transformation that occurred through the work of our imagination, blending the experience of the moment with the embedded memories of images and symbols given by our culture and traditions.

Both examples show culturally learned patterns of behavior, the first more "narrative" or story-based than the second. But also note that in the first example, the walk along the way of the cross also had a directional quality to it, a path that was trod, a beginning and an end. The second example was pure learned symbolic gesture that elicited a sense of divine presence and prayerful communion by its association with a sacred and peaceful greeting from another culture. But even that learned gesture had a certain bodily orientation, with Driver moving his hands, palms together, downward and feeling "centered" in that action.

The Imagination at Work through Our Bodies

Both of the stories above show that there is a certain knowing, a certain opening up onto reality that is particular to the bodies we inhabit. We are whole creatures, using our imaginations to create a world of symbolic meaning rooted in our bodily experience. In the preface to his

5. Tom Driver, *Liberating Rites* (Boulder, Colo.: Westview Press, 1998), p. 96.

book *The Body in the Mind,* Mark Johnson writes that "without imagination, nothing in the world could be meaningful. Without imagination, we could never make sense of our experience. Without imagination, we could never reason toward knowledge of reality."[6] Johnson is particularly concerned with images and metaphors grounded in bodily experience, out of which first emerges our understanding of what is real and true about ourselves and the world around us.

Specifically, you have a body. You probably cannot imagine what it would be like not to have this body that you inhabit, whatever its current shape! From your earliest infancy, from the moment you began to reach for that mobile above your crib, you began to develop a sense of spatial orientation, a sense of far versus near. From the time you began to crawl, you developed a sense of the space about you, more abstract mental "maps" of the world you inhabit — you began to grasp a meaning of present versus absent, a sense of in versus out. And when you started to pull yourself to your feet, you developed sensory-motor "maps," those more complex mental models based on your interactions with the world about you — for example, a sense of up versus down and balance versus imbalance — that organized your grasp of reality.

As you developed language skills and the ability to interact verbally with others in your environment, your experience began also to be conceptually shaped by your family and culture and the historical time in which you live. And all of these sources of experience fed into an overall grasp of your world as a whole. In short, your whole sense of reality emerged experientially and metaphorically out of an embodied base of "imaginary maps," giving coherence and structure to your experience. The point here is that your bodily engagement with the world grounds this whole background network, and the power of your imagination creates a world of meaning rooted in this experience.

Johnson discusses a number of basic imaginary mappings that have their source in our bodily experience. In order to clarify what we're

6. Mark Johnson, *The Body in the Mind* (Chicago: University of Chicago Press, 1987), p. ix. In this discussion I am indebted to Johnson, who also co-authored a second volume with his colleague George Lakoff entitled *Metaphors We Live By,* cited earlier. The field of ritual studies is a vast one, and I could have chosen any number of possible routes into it. But I have chosen Johnson's route because of its consistency with the theme of this book, and because there is something convincing and thus elegant in his treatment of embodied meaning in our lives.

talking about here, I'll use his discussion of *path* as an example of such mental mappings.

Johnson begins his discussion of mental path maps by pointing out that our lives are filled with paths that connect the spatial world around us. There's a path from our bed to our closet, from our front door to our office, from California to New York. And there are some paths that exist only in our imagination — for example, the path that connects the earth with whatever exists beyond our solar system or beyond the farthest known galaxy.

Beneath all of these examples is a single recurring map pattern with an imagined starting point, a goal, and a sequential pattern connecting start with finish. In other words, paths move us from one point to another. Johnson further points out that since these schematic paths are *human* paths, they generally are purposive in nature and thus tend to be directional or goal-oriented rather than non-directional.

Out of this basic directional and purposive path-mapping, based on our human experience of physical locomotion, our imaginations create symbolic and metaphorical elaborations that connote human meaning and expression, as well as goal-driven behavior. So such expressions as "I've got quite a ways to go before I make my quota" and "She's gotten sidetracked halfway through her course of study" represent elaborations of basic embodied image mappings. If you recall my story of walking the Via Dolorosa, you will see, for example, that the whole concept of pilgrimage becomes a spatially and temporally extended metaphorical elaboration of a goal-directed path map based fundamentally on embodied symbolic meaning, my experience of moving from here to there for a purpose.

Thus metaphor represents a second type of imaginative element in Johnson's writings. As Johnson sees it, metaphors frequently represent these embodied mappings imaginatively projected and elaborated in both actions and language. Because of their actual embodied base of meaning, such metaphorical elaborations also limit the metaphorical implications that can be drawn out and used to convey meaning in conversation with others. We can't just imaginatively create metaphors willy-nilly and have them make sense when we talk with each other. Metaphors "fit" because they are consistent with how our body and the world works, how our experience has gotten built up over years of moving and sensing and learning. "*Follow my lead* in this argument" makes more metaphorical sense than *"Follow my cushion* in this argument." In the first sentence, "follow my lead" implies moving toward some hoped-for goal; in the second sentence, "follow my cushion" conveys no socially shared meaning for goal-directed behavior. The metaphor just doesn't work because it lies outside the bounds of our experience.

In fact, you and I are embedded in an interpersonal, shared world of meaning, and so we're not just talking here about individual understanding of our own reality. We're talking about a sense of reality and socially grounded meaning communally imagined and shared by members of a group. In this way, the world we inhabit is mutually intelligible as we act jointly and speak together in community.

Finally, the way you and I understand the world around us is the result of our total experience, the complex *blending* of all the input from our culture, our personal and social history, and our bodily based image maps, all fitting together and undergirding our sense of what is real and true. And all of this total grasping — this creative blending — is a function of our imaginative capacity, this same power that Coleridge and others have characterized as our essential human capacity to perceive and create meaning around us. According to Johnson, our bodily engagement with the world grounds this foundational network, and the power of our imagination creates a world of meaning founded on it.

Again, a basic assumption in this present discussion is that God or the transcendent Other intrudes or impinges on this imaginative capacity, opening up and revealing the deepest truths of our lives. As Coleridge put it, as symbol-makers we meet the Symbol Giver in the creative, imaginative act. And I have explored Johnson's ideas to underscore my point that imagination and its God-given power to create meaning lie at the heart of it all.

Ritual and Story

These imaginary maps we have been discussing, rooted in our body's sense of orientation and blended into our background of everyday meaning, also become metaphorically elaborated into religious rites and liturgical concepts. For example, "up" experienced as "higher" (e.g., the toddler reaches "up" to get the cookie lying on the "high" tabletop) becomes metaphorically extended in our conceptual understanding of God as a transcendent, "higher" Being, and of heaven as a "higher" realm somehow metaphorically "above" us mortals; conversely, we bow "down" before the transcendent Being we worship. Thus rites are seen as embodied sequences of actions, structured in terms of these natural, physical dimensions of our experience and given meaning by the believing community's stories, myths, and parables.

Recall that in my walking of the Via Dolorosa, an abstract map founded on my experience of *path* became metaphorically extended to mean a journey retracing the steps of Christ. Similarly, our experience of *cycles* or cyclic change — the coming and going of seasons, the cyclic repetitions of bodily functions (e.g., cycles of sleeping and waking) — provide imaginary mappings or paradigms for liturgical cycles, for the yearly celebration of feasts, saints' festivals, and fasts of all the major religious systems.

Our whole existence as human beings is mediated by both body and mind. Thus the embodied symbols expressed in ritual and the meaning of our lives shaped by story are essentially linked. As Herbert Anderson and Edward Foley put it, "Ritual is embodied expression, and narrative springs from the human imagination," which is grounded in embodied experience. "Rituals shape our stories, and our instinct to perceive life as a narrative urges us to rehearse that narrative through our bodies."[7] We are whole beings, truly flesh and spirit.

What might be helpful here is another example of individual ritual, again with metaphorical and narrative meaning shaped by the religious community.

When I was about eighteen, I spent the summer studying French at Laval University in Quebec. One Saturday I took a bus out to the shrine of Sainte-Anne-de-Beaupré. Though other details of that trip have faded, one experience remains vividly in my mind.

There was a shrine on the grounds — maybe it was the main shrine, I don't know. But it was a popular place for devotion, because lines of the devout waited to approach that sacred space. What I remember is that the shrine was located in a grotto, at the top of a long

---

7. Herbert Anderson and Edward Foley, *Mighty Stories, Dangerous Rituals* (San Francisco: Jossey-Bass, 1998), p. 27.

flight of stairs. And the faithful — most of them, at any rate, those who could — were climbing the stairs on their knees as a sign of penitence and piety. The women were holding rosaries in their hands and wearing mantillas over their heads. And I remember joining that throng that day, also making my way up those stairs on my knees.

Reflecting on this stair-climbing ritual, I think that the embodied mapping and the metaphorical elaborations involved included the experience of "up" versus "down," as well as "path" as a way to a sacred physical and spiritual goal. Certainly the stairs represented an ascent, physically and metaphorically, because the way was hard and steep. The sacred story of the Via Crucis shaped the narrative meaning for the difficult climb and the journey. In fact, the entire pilgrimage could be seen as founded on my imaginary map or sense of a path or a way to somewhere important. Metaphorically and conceptually, the visit to that shrine became a way to holiness and sanctification as I undertook that difficult ascent.

All the major world religions — Hinduism, Buddhism, Judaism, Islam, and Christianity — incorporate the notion of pilgrimage as part of their devotional systems. A pilgrimage to Jerusalem, for example, retraces the life and steps of the founder of that faith in some sense. For the Christian, the basic metaphor giving shape and meaning to the pilgrim's way is the way of the cross embedded within the story of Gospel salvation. In tracing the arduous path to sanctity, the individual pilgrim suffers and walks with Christ metaphorically and imaginatively.

So, as Richard Niebuhr put it, "Pilgrims are persons in motion — passing through territories not their own, seeking something we might call completion . . . a goal to which only the spirit's compass points the way."[8] And so, on that long-ago pilgrimage to Sainte-Anne-de-Beaupré, and more recently, during a week-long visit to the holy island of Iona, Scotland, I (along with many others) have embarked on pathways through territory imaginatively given meaning by myth and story imparted by the religious community. I have embarked on these and other journeys in order to continue — through the power of my imagination — the task of creating and defining myself, not alone, but in the com-

8. Richard Niebuhr, quoted in Nora Gallagher, *Things Seen and Unseen* (New York: Alfred A. Knopf, 1998), p. 163.

pany of Another who calls me to do so. Anderson and Foley express it this way: "In our rituals, like our stories, we narrate our existence, that is to say, we individually and collectively express and create a vision of life."[9]

Communal Ritual and the Corporate Imagination

Up until now, our focus for the most part has been on individual ritualistic actions reflecting a world of meaning shaped by our community. At the center of this world of meaning is the individual's imaginative capacity, which creates a world of meaning by a blending and a sense-making of experience at all levels, from the physical to the cultural. The background of this taken-for-granted reality is drawn from one's bodily perception and developed by metaphor and concepts absorbed and learned from one's historical context.

Social groups, including religious communities, are powerful shapers of experienced reality. But at the core of communities, perhaps basic to all community, lies a common generic bond of humanity, a basic sense of belonging to a human community, a basic sense of "human being–ness" that we all share deep in our imaginative core. Although that background sense of shared humanity becomes shaped by our particular community, underneath the stories and the myths and the ideology lies this common human core.

If you recall the opening of this chapter and my description of the night of 9/11 — the gathering of people at St. Mark's that night whether they were "religious" or not, whether they were believers or not — you will also see that that gathering reflected this sense of a common human bond that lies beneath our various social and cultural differences. In extremis, when our country is attacked, when a hurricane devastates a city, when a planet-shaking disaster like a tsunami wipes away a part of our world, we fall back on what is common to us all because, as John Donne wrote, "the bell tolls for thee." Perhaps that is why the looting and general mayhem that also sometimes occur under those extreme conditions are so shocking to most of us. The looters seem somehow outside the bonds of humanity, outside that common

9. Anderson and Foley, *Mighty Stories, Dangerous Rituals,* p. 26.

bond that becomes so apparent when our collective backs are against the wall.

Community and Transformation

Now what does all this have to do with ritual, imagination, and faith development? The answer lies in our previous discussion of Johnson and Lakoff's work. Our background sense of reality develops as our imagination "blends" our bodily experience with meaning given and shaped by our community's stories, its culture, its history. It is in the imagination of the participants that such a transformed sense of their world becomes real, becomes the experienced background of reality shared with others in community. If such a transformation occurs within a context replete with religious symbols and stories, the shared background experienced is religious in nature.

Although the ritual acts that we perform are inseparable from the community that shapes their meaning, *there is something about doing the thing itself,* something about literally standing up and being counted or publicly putting your body on the line, that is or can be transformative in itself. In fact, bodily actions can be a very powerful way to define the self, not only for others but for the one performing them. Roy Rappaport notes, "As 'saying' may be 'doing,' 'doing' may also be an especially powerful — or substantial — way of 'saying.'"[10] Kneeling, processing, making a sign of the cross, touching a passing Torah scroll — such ritual acts and gestures convey something more than mere words. The saying that "actions speak louder than words" is surely true. Actions also convey undeniably concrete messages. You stand to be counted; you kneel or you don't.

A specific example will help to make my point. In his introduction to *The Future of Ritual,* Richard Schechner describes a ritual that he participated in during a visit to India in 1976. Ethnically Jewish, he decided to undergo a conversion rite, primarily to gain easy access to Hindu temples for study. The night before the ritual, he struggled with

10. Roy Rappaport, "The Obvious Aspects of Ritual," from *Ecology, Meaning, and Religion,* reprinted in *Readings in Ritual Studies,* ed. Ronald L. Grimes (Upper Saddle River, N.J.: Prentice Hall, Inc., 1996), p. 436.

what he was doing, because he didn't want to lose his "Jewishness" in the process. For him the rite was an instrumental means to access; nevertheless, he knew the power of ritual acts to convey meaning to the self as well as to others. Ultimately he decided to go through with it, and he describes the ritual itself:

> The next morning the initiation was performed. . . . I repeated the many mantras I was instructed to enunciate. The sacred thread was laid over my left shoulder. Sandal paste was applied to my forehead. I was given my Hindu name. At the end of it all, I received a small "Conversion Certificate."[11]

Schechner goes on to explain what he learned that day despite his less-than-authentic conversion: that ritual acts are very powerful even if there is some measure of duplicity in undertaking them. He says that to this day he keeps his sacred thread, because in some way he had "performed himself into" at least a partial new identity, that of a Jewish-Hindu male.

Humans do show the startling ability to create themselves through such ritualistic acts as Schechner describes (one becomes a ballet dancer by dancing ballet; one truly becomes a priest by performing the mass). But in the end, such public ritual acts in the absence of a larger sense of narrative meaning may be quite fragile.

What then is authentic ritual? And where does God or a transcendent Being fit into all of this? Let's begin with the first of these two questions.

Authentic Ritual

As we discussed in the introduction, out of our taken-for-granted, everyday background of experience, our imagination creates myths, rituals, art, poetry, and philosophies that speak to this background experience of what is real. When ritual is authentic, it arises out of this background and expresses genuine meaning beyond what our words can say. Think back to the story of Tom Driver standing at his kitchen

---

11. Richard Schechner, *The Future of Ritual* (New York: Routledge, 1993), p. 4.

stove in the early morning and folding his hands in prayer. That ritual gesture expressed a deep sense of connection with God at that moment. He couldn't put it into words, but through ritual he expressed and fleshed out — literally — his sense of his God-inhabited world at that moment.

When this powerful background sense is experienced in community and reflected in fitting ritual actions, there is a kind of effervescence or flow that's experienced by those caught up in the embodied expression. In the early twentieth century, Émile Durkheim described such an experience as a feeling of being transformed in ritual doing, of being swept away by some external force that moves and transforms the ritual participants. Others speak of "flow" in similar terms, describing it as a "holistic sensation present when we act with total involvement . . . experienced . . . in artistic performance and religious ritual";[12] it is a sense of being caught up in oneness with others and with Something or Someone beyond the collective selves. For those of you who remember the 1960s, the phrase "Go with the flow" referred to just this sense of free-flowing, unself-conscious experience.

Music and Ritual

There is not space here to examine in depth the role that music plays in speaking to this deep level of human experience, stirring some depths of meaning beyond words. But music that moves us does indeed touch us at our very core. Some music experienced in community, out of lived and shared human meaning, vibrates and stirs up within us this effervescence that Durkheim described, providing perhaps another access to Transcendence distinct from other creations such as story or visual art.[13] Tom Driver describes his experience of listening to voodoo drumming through headphones while sitting at his desk one day. When he got up to walk down the hall, he realized that he was "quite high," not

12. Victor Turner and Edith Turner, *Image and Pilgrimage in Christian Culture* (New York: Columbia University Press, 1978), p. 254.

13. As we will see in Chapter Two, poetry also has a "musical," rhythmic quality to it. But poetry is also a literary creation with elements and form distinct from other imaginative products, affording its own unique opening onto Transcendent mystery.

34

from chemicals but from the rhythm of the drums vibrating through his head and soul.[14]

George Steiner says that music can literally madden, console, exalt, heal — it expresses meaning beyond what can be said. Music is "somatic, carnal and a searching out of resonances in our bodies at levels deeper than will or consciousness." He also says that when we are caught up in the experience of music that stirs us and sweeps us up into its power, there lies a hint of some Beyond, some radical "non-humanity . . . intimations of a source and destination somehow outside the range of man."[15] Such music indeed speaks to the mystery of transcendent intrusions into our world of experience.

On the evening of the first anniversary of 9/11, the community again gathered at St. Mark's Church. We began the service with a brass orchestra playing Aaron Copland's *Fanfare for the Common Man*. It is hard to describe how incredibly moving the experience of that music was on that fateful night. In our coming together to express in ritual form our common humanity and our solidarity with each other and with those who had died, that musical prelude to what followed captured our shared humanity in a way that words could not.

So authentic ritual springs from and expresses our deepest human meaning out of this embodied, shared ground of experience. Authentic ritual speaks from this depth. But again, the symbols of institutional community (the language, culture, myths, and metaphors that belong to the tradition of the community — in our case, the religious community) are also essential. Imagination unmoored, imagination run amok, without anchor in a communal culture that conveys moral, ethical, and theological meaning, can end in unstructured chaos — end sometimes even in the diabolical rituals of a Jonestown or the Branch Davidians of Waco, Texas.

This is a good place to consider more fully the *development* of com-

---

14. Driver, *Liberating Rites,* p. 61. Like ritual, the desire to make music and to move rhythmically in dance seems to be hardwired into us humans. Barbara Ehrenreich has written a lively book on communal celebration, *Dancing in the Street* (New York: Henry Holt & Company, 2006), which expounds on this inborn drive to make festive expressions in group gatherings.

15. George Steiner, *Real Presences* (Chicago: University of Chicago Press, 1989), pp. 197, 217.

munity ritual, before turning finally to the question of meeting God in our imaginative ritual actions.

The Development of Communal Ritual

In the beginning of our discussion about ritual, I made the point that we share with lower forms of animal life an innate need to engage in ritual actions. Unlike the rituals of your dog or cat or canary, however, most of the rituals that you and I engage in, their particular form and metaphorical meaning, are learned. Hence, in the matter of religious rituals, the conceptual meaning of the rites we engage in are shaped and imparted by religious traditions.

Particular rituals themselves belong to history, to the time and culture that gives them shape and meaning. As Tom Driver explains, "Agents of transformation, rituals are themselves transformed by their histories to which they belong."[16] Without such authentic development of ritual to express our current, lived meaning, ritual forms become hardened and dead. When the community institutions — the church, the hierarchy, the religious powers that be — suppress the free expression of new ritual, rigidity sets in. And without a dynamic process shaping a coherent ritual life, the vision of any community, religious or otherwise, becomes banal.

Thus, our most treasured rites, if they speak to the meaning of our lives as we live them, remain dynamic only if they continue to fit our actual experience blended by the power of our imagination — that background experience which we bring to the communal gathering. The opening of a Holocaust memorial with ritual solemnity expresses the deepest sense of sacred community for those who remember. The lighting of the memorial flame at the site of the Hiroshima bombing, the annual remembrance of 9/11, the throwing of a fistful of dirt on an open grave by those gathered around, the carrying of the Olympic torch — all these ritual forms express in bodily action the meaning now lived and the hope now conceptualized by the community's stories and metaphors.

Perhaps, in the last analysis, authentic ritual is experienced and enacted by participants when the stories that give them narrative signifi-

---

16. Driver, *Liberating Rites,* p. 184.

cance touch their very lives at the deepest level — at that level of experienced meaning that is finally beyond saying and must be imaginatively expressed in music and gesture. In religious terms, the ritual practice becomes fitting when the story of our lives in its lived fullness intersects with the divine story told and re-enacted in the liturgy. Let's look at a prime example of such liturgy.

Ritual, Memory, and Enacted Story: The Centrality of the Feast

Ritual action — processing with the Torah scroll, bowing to a cross in procession, climbing stairs to a shrine on one's knees, lying prone and covered by a shroud during a monastic profession, eating a Seder meal, building a prayer hut for the feast of Purim — forms the symbolic base for the liturgical text, the Scripture story conceptualized and informed by theological reflection within various traditions. This text, in turn, informs the ritual action or rite, allowing the participants to come to a fuller, more articulated understanding of what the religious rite means.

Thus, the ritual and the text are mutually dependent for their intelligibility, communicating meaning and doing something that complements and deepens the meaning for the participants. And it is the imagination of the participants that creates and recreates this experience as they re-enact the story and express the meaning of the worship by doing the ritual action.

Let's look at one key example of such interplay between word and action: the meal as sacred sacrament. My focus here will necessarily be on the Christian rite because this is the one most familiar to me. But first I'll trace its roots, which are buried deep in the ancient Jewish Passover ritual, grounded in Jewish Scripture and history.

The Jewish Passover Ritual

The story of the exodus of the Jewish people from slavery in Egypt is recorded in biblical history (in the twelfth chapter of the book of Exodus). The Passover ritual that evolved as a memorial to that event is thought by some to have originated in pagan rites of nomadic tribes, celebrating new life and ensuring the well-being of their flocks by an annual sacrifice. However it originated, the Passover meal memorialized that escape from slavery through God's intervention. But the meal also came to symbolize much more than that.

Participants relived the original Exodus passage in the meal rite, dressed as if ready for a journey, consuming unleavened bread as if in haste to depart that land of bondage. Cups of wine were blessed and drunk, symbolizing Israelite joy at the mighty saving deeds of God (Exod. 6:6-7). But the fifth, undrunk cup of wine (the Cup of Elijah) symbolized the final promise of God to his people, that great day of the Lord when final salvation will occur, ushered in by the coming again of the great prophet Elijah.

These and other ritual gestures were accompanied by words spoken by the father or head male at the feast, explaining the meaning of the meal and blessing God for his saving acts. These words of the liturgy thus flesh out the meaning of the action, creating in the imagination of those gathered a vital remembering, a reliving, a realizing in thought and feeling of the meaning of the Exodus event, here recreated anew.

The Last Supper of Jesus

Scholars debate whether Jesus and his disciples celebrated an actual Passover meal on the night he was betrayed, or whether this last supper was held the night before Passover, as part of his customary meal held with his closest friends for purposes of prayer and communal fellowship. I lean toward those who subscribe to the latter, following the order of events found in the Gospel of John.

In any event, table fellowship and, indeed, the acts of eating and drinking as metaphorical expression were central to Jesus' ministry. Anderson and Foley refer to Jesus as "a storyteller with bread,"[17] and I think that is a wonderfully apt image for Jesus' years of active ministry as recorded in Scripture.

Jesus' whole public ministry was indeed framed by ritual meals, beginning, as John tells it, with the wedding feast at Cana and ending with Jesus' last supper with his closest followers. In between, he dined with tax collectors and prostitutes, as well as with more respectable

17. Anderson and Foley, *Mighty Stories, Dangerous Rituals,* p. 154.

38

members of the Jewish community. One memorable scene in Scripture has him reclining at the dinner table when a prostitute (Mary Magdalene) pours precious oil on his feet (symbolizing his coming death and burial), bathing them with her tears.

Jesus linked the ritual of eating and table fellowship with forgiveness of sins, acceptance, and reconciliation. Indeed, he likened the kingdom of God — that final salvation of all creation, gathered up into God's final blessing — to a great feast where all will be invited to partake. This final vision is one of brotherhood and sisterhood for all saved by God's mercy, the least and the poorest and the marginal to be included first in God's saving scheme.

It is not surprising, then, that Jesus spent his last night with his disciples in table fellowship and prayer. Whether this was a Passover supper or a customary supper fellowship with his friends, Jesus instituted a new ritual that night — not a new ritual act of sharing bread and wine, but a new ritual *meaning* in the sharing. He said, "Do this in memory of me." Do this in memory of my coming death. Do this in memory of my sacrifice poured out for you and for all. To this day Jesus' followers have done this, with its new meaning of forgiveness and salvation, looking forward to the final feast of wholeness at the close of history.

This meal and all that it symbolizes is at the heart, the core of the Christian tradition. Just as those gathered at a Seder meal re-experience in their imagination the saving events of the Exodus, so those who gather for a communion service, no matter what their particular denomination, imaginatively relive this pivotal last supper and re-experience life amid death. Anderson and Foley comment, "This meal, fashioned in the image of Jesus' whole ministry and recalled in every Christian Eucharist, is a place where death is sampled in a loaf of bread; where tasting wine imperils life as we know it. . . . Here is where belief is tested and faith is forged."[18]

The Meal as Embodied Metaphor

From our earliest years, the bodily acts of eating and drinking are experienced as vital to life, as the means of nourishment that are primary to our survival. Based on this embodied experience, metaphorical mean-

---

18. Anderson and Foley, *Mighty Stories, Dangerous Rituals,* pp. 156-57.

ing becomes elaborated, founded on a shared communal understanding of consumption and sustenance. A variety of expressions — "I can't digest this fact," "He swallowed that lie whole," "I'm hungry for knowledge," "She consumes me and my time," "I could devour him with my eyes" — represent metaphorical expressions based on this primary image-mapping, to use Mark Johnson's terminology. In eating the sacramental bread and wine, in taking in symbolic nourishment for our soul, we survive and thrive by partaking of the sacred communal meal. We take in, we are nourished, and we are transformed by the bread and wine, physically and symbolically. Truly, you and I are what we eat.

Sunday after Sunday, season in and season out, this belief is shaped and nurtured. The storytelling and the ritual acts of the Christian community come together to forge this faith even in the face of doubt and failure and tragic circumstance — in shared crises such as the night of 9/11 and in our day-to-day struggles for emotional survival. The divine story and the human story, the community's story and the individual's existential, embodied experience of hunger as well as pain, suffering, and the need for reconciliation and forgiveness, the longing for salvation and brotherhood and sisterhood — this background meaning of our shared humankind-ness finds ritual expression.

My point here is this: The religious community (here within the Christian tradition) could not survive without our imagination's weaving of these stories into a complex of embodied symbols expressed in ritual. As Anderson and Foley remind us, the Lord's Supper is the ultimate embodiment of the Christian story. And our imaginative engagement with it lies at the core of our faith development.

However, as I suggested earlier, the tradition's stories do not always speak to the lived story of our own lives. Such disconnection can occur when the music and its lyrics are flaccid and spiritless, when ritualistic expression is discouraged, when liturgical forms lack energy, or when the stories embodied in the sermons are irrelevant. When that disjunction happens, rituals grow cold and dead. When the community stories that impart meaning to the ritual acts no longer speak to our background condition, such acts become rote, and restless boredom sets in.

It remains true that the acts performed — eating, drinking, standing, kneeling, processing, folding hands, singing songs of joy and sorrow — have their own integrity and convey their own corporal meaning. But the experience can be truncated because the divine story and the human stories no longer connect very well, or because the community and its rigid strictures have stifled authentic expression.

But at their best, in vital Eucharistic celebrations or lively Seder meals, when rituals shaped by sacred stories and songs touch our deepest needs for life and wholeness, we do narrate our existence, as persons and as a religious community. We express meaning, and in the expressing we create a whole vision of life. Again, both this embodied, metaphorical expressing and our human and divine storytelling emerge out of our imagination. As Anderson and Foley put it, "Rituals shape our stories, and our instinct to perceive life as a narrative urges us to rehearse that narrative through our bodies."[19] And thus we shape our world.

Ritual and the Transcendent: Meeting God in Ritual Acts

"Without imagination, nothing in the world could be meaningful. Without imagination, we could never make sense of our experience. Without imagination, we could never reason toward knowledge of reality."[20] These sweeping statements from Mark Johnson, which make up one of the epigraphs you encountered earlier, speak to the essence not only of this chapter but of this entire book. With Johnson, we traced out an understanding of reality grounded in our bodily experience of making our way in the world. We saw that ritual acts are one form of symbolic elaboration and extension of our experienced reality, of our background understanding of what is real and true in the world about us. Reaching out through the creative power of our imagination, we glimpse traces of God in the process.

George Steiner, near the end of his *Real Presences,* argues for what he calls a "wager on transcendence." He argues that in the genuine engagement with an imaginative creation — ritual action, poetic expression, visual art, music, story — there is a grasp of ultimate meaning, a "presumption of presence." You can refuse this open engagement (you

19. Anderson and Foley, *Mighty Stories, Dangerous Rituals,* p. 27.
20. Johnson, *The Body in the Mind,* p. ix.

can keep the imagination's gate shut tight) by various means — by not being attuned to such hints of transcendent Presence, by refusing to be open to it. But Steiner, also echoing Coleridge, says that there should be no mistake. All of these symbolic expressions are reincarnations of God's originating creative fiat, and are thus affirmations of some transcendent Reality at work in our lives. Such imaginative expressions, he says, make us "close neighbours to the transcendent. Poetry, art, music are the medium of that neighborhood."[21]

As we have seen, genuine ritualistic acts within the context of a religion's myths and metaphors are embodied symbols expressing our deepest core meaning. Such meaning includes a longing for reconciliation and wholeness, a basic longing to encounter this divine Transcendence penetrating and infusing our world. But the point here is that our embodied humanness — our bodily experience — is one of imagination's gateways opening onto the divine.

*   *   *

I began this chapter by focusing on the aftermath of 9/11, the gathering that night at St. Mark's in response to our nation's crisis, the experience of genuine community, a shared human kindness, the felt need for communal, ritual expression in the face of suffering and loss, and the meaning such ritual helps us create.

But most of our lives are lived in ordinary time, in the mundane, day-to-day struggle of jobs and relationships and kids and bills. Most of the time we live in an arid wasteland where we strain to hear the word of God in our daily lives, searching out some ray of transcendent hope for life beyond death.

In a beautiful set of images to which we'll return from time to time, George Steiner weaves the metaphor of "Saturday." He says we all know about Good Friday in our lives — we all know pain and suffering and betrayal and death. And we all hope for an Easter Sunday of resurrection, hope for a future beyond this "vale of tears," for some place that is home, for some healing and wholeness we can trust. But in the meantime, we live in "the long Saturday." Between the suffering and the liberation there is our daily life. Steiner says, "In the death of love

21. Steiner, *Real Presences*, p. 215.

that is Friday, even the greatest art and poetry are almost helpless."[22] Almost, but not quite, because traces of transcendent Presence can be gleaned in our God-graced creative acts — our acts of ritual expression, our aesthetic acts of poetry-writing and storytelling. The option remains open for living whole lives by embracing on all levels our human story as it intersects with the divine, imaginatively creating and shaping our becoming in the process. It seems to me that this is the only true option that you and I have.

22. Steiner, *Real Presences,* pp. 231-32.

CHAPTER TWO

Meeting God in Poetry and Visual Art:
The Power of Metaphor and Symbol

> *The Sea of Faith*
> *Was once, too, at the full, and round earth's shore*
> *. . . But now I only hear*
> *Its melancholy, long, withdrawing roar,*
> *Retreating, to the breath*
> *Of the night-wind, down the vast edges drear*
> *And naked shingles of the world.*
>
> Matthew Arnold, "Dover Beach"

In Ian McEwan's novel *Saturday*,[1] the climax of his spellbinding plot begins when a deranged killer named Baxter holds a knife to the throat of the wife of the main character, Henry. Having broken into Henry's home during a family gathering, Baxter and his criminal sidekick have just forced Henry's daughter Daisy to disrobe and then read something from the book of poems she has with her. And so, shaking, she reads Matthew Arnold's poignant lament, "Dover Beach."

And then, suddenly, Baxter appears "elated," radiant, almost giddy with joy and excitement. With mercurial swiftness, he changes his mind about rape and murder as he pockets his knife. He mistakenly assumes that Daisy herself could actually have created such a beautiful piece. He exclaims, "How could you have thought of that? I mean, you just wrote

---

1. Ian McEwan, *Saturday* (New York: Doubleday, 2005).

it." And then he says it again, several times over. "You wrote it!" The poem seems to have touched some nostalgic memory ("It makes me think of where I grew up," he says), some meaningful image in Baxter's life. In this novel, Arnold's poem seems to have had at least a momentary salvific effect on Baxter, triggering some labile, positive response in his damaged brain. Such, in McEwan's story, is the power of poetry to touch lives, casting "a spell on one man," transfixing him.[2]

Arnold probably wrote "Dover Beach" during the 1850s, and as a whole — and in its historical, cultural context — it does seem to express a melancholy mourning for a lost world of firm faith. In fact, along with other poets such as Tennyson and Baudelaire, Arnold is credited with "sounding the first mournful notes of what would become modernism,"[3] a modern/post-modern world that you and I now inhabit.

Since I think it's important to situate the poets and other artists whom we will discuss in this chapter within some kind of historical framework, I will sketch very briefly — and therefore, very generally — the path that art has followed in the modern Western world.

Romanticism to Postmodernism in Poetry and Visual Art

The Romantics of the nineteenth century, including Coleridge, Wordsworth, and others, viewed the creative imagination as a meeting place between God and humans, inspired by divine breath. This meeting and

---

2. McEwan, *Saturday*, p. 288. I find the title of McEwan's work intriguing. We ended the previous chapter on ritual with a reference to George Steiner's metaphorical use of the notion of Saturday as that time in between the Good Friday pain of our lives and the hope of a Resurrection Sunday, a place beyond this "vale of tears," a place of homecoming and *shalom*. In the meantime, we live in the long Saturday of life, between suffering and liberation. I closed that chapter by quoting Steiner: "In the death of love that is Friday, even the greatest art and poetry are almost helpless." And I added, "Almost, but not quite." For God's transcendent Presence can be imaginatively glimpsed and gleaned through the creative making of aesthetic works such as poems and visual art, as well as through active engagement with such creative products. And of course, that is the topic of this present chapter.

3. Peggy Rosenthal, *The Poets' Jesus* (New York: Oxford University Press, 2000), p. 53. I am indebted to this writer's commentary on the modern and postmodern poets whom we consider in this chapter.

thus disclosure of the Divine was most perfectly expressed through poetic form. But on the same historical stage where the Romantics were celebrating the individual's imaginative power as an opening onto the Transcendent, the Industrial Revolution, with all its dehumanizing effects, was holding sway. And in many artists and intellectuals of that day it triggered an experience of divine withdrawal leading to a sense of hopelessness. The horrors of urban poverty and disease, along with a world war and its aftermath of disillusionment, led to both pessimism and protest.

On the religious front, many scholars joined in the celebration of human progress through scientific discovery and the promise of capitalistic progress. However, the effects of higher biblical criticism, tracing the historical and human development of the Bible, tended to undermine simple religious faith. In addition, Christianity's search for the "historical Jesus," with its focus on his humanity and life in history, also served to empty out the mystery of the sacred, weakening traditional Western religious beliefs.

All of these forces, even the humanistic ones that exulted in cultural progress and the "divinity" of individual consciousness (e.g., Walt Whitman's celebration of the "self" in his poetry and Emerson's vision of each human as sharing in divinity in some way) — these modern forces had an eroding effect on traditional religious certitude in general and on orthodox religious faith in particular.

Overall, therefore, by the twentieth century, what had begun as a celebration of enlightened humanism and human potential, along with an optimistic, romantic idealization of the individual within Western culture, seemed finally to turn foul (as one writer puts it) as the combined effects of war, poverty, greed, and corruption became apparent. Thus, in the arts, alienation, pessimism, and cynicism, along with a sometimes-defiant spirit of humanistic protest, appeared in word and image.

By the mid-twentieth century, T. S. Eliot's *The Waste Land* and Samuel Beckett's *Waiting for Godot* expressed this landscape of disenchantment, the "hollow core of the human condition." As Peggy Rosenthal observes, we hear Beckett's "play's refrain 'if Godot [or God] comes, we'll be saved.' But he doesn't, so they just wait."[4] Thus, the earlier sad-

---

4. Rosenthal, *The Poets' Jesus*, p. 112.

ness of a Matthew Arnold, lamenting the loss of certitude in the modern world, had at least partially given way to cynicism and despair over the human ability to know anything true at all. The Romantic's trust in the bond of truth between the human word and the world of reality had been broken.

Finally, this lack of any deep meaning, this inability to make sense of life in any comprehensive way, ceased even to be mourned by many. As Rosenthal notes, there emerged a loss even of the *sense* of transcendent loss. Thus, the artworks that were created out of this worldview became absolutely secular in nature, even if the subject matter happened to have historical religious roots. Rosenthal puts it this way:

> A culture must make meaning for its members; a culture in fact is, by some definitions, the system of signs carrying meaning for a given society. The secularized West recognized itself in crisis because it had dispensed with its inherited belief system, yet had no other at hand to make sense of human existence.[5]

It seemed that neither language nor visual symbol could speak or grasp any transcendent meaning, and mere bewilderment was left in the wake. In the remaining vacuum, the imagination of the artist became the creative source of meaning and human redemption. Visual art — the paintings of a Klee or a Kandinsky — became art for art's sake, with its highest purpose being aesthetic contemplation of the world created by the artist's own elevated, god-like subjectivity.

As Rosenthal points out, the movement from modernism's "melancholy moan" — where God seemed to be gone from the world's stage and no one seemed to know exactly why — to postmodernism's triumph of secular humanism is not clearly demarcated. Nor has God remained completely in the wings as the scene has shifted. Hints and glimpses of the Infinite have continued to shine obliquely through the limits of language and visual signs throughout the modern era.

In fact, it has been argued by some that the contemporary, postmodern scene is not only conducive to humanistic exploration because it frees the mind from religious absolutes, but is also conducive to asking ultimate questions and exploring the limits of human knowledge

---

5. Rosenthal, *The Poets' Jesus*, p. 72.

within a world of pluralistic perspectives. For at least some, this freedom from the moorings of traditional orthodoxy has opened up a new quest for some transcendent meaning in our spiritually hungry age.

In the introduction, I discussed Douglas Coupland's characterization of his Generation X and how they're starting from zero — those who were raised in a culture "after God." He considers that culture in his book *Life after God,* in which one of his characters muses,

> Life was charmed but without politics or religion. It was the life of children of the children of the pioneers — life after God — a life of earthly salvation on the edge of heaven. . . . We gained an irony that scorched everything it touched. And I wonder if this irony is the price we paid for the loss of God. But then I must remind myself we are living creatures — we have religious impulses — we *must* — and yet into what cracks do these impulses flow in a world without religion? It is something I think about every day.[6]

The poetry and visual artworks that we will take up in this chapter all reflect this longing for the Transcendent. Not every artist would subscribe to the idea of the Transcendent as a source of inspiration. But all artists live with and experience mystery; all experience that moment when they are seemingly seized by some external force and led into unknown paths of discovery and creativity.

This search for God or the wholly Other — despite the rampant secularism of our age and the cynicism of our contemporary culture — has never absented itself for long from our contemporary world. It is the premise of this book that we all have "religious impulses." And through our imaginative engagement with poetic and visual art, both as creators and as receivers of such works, we do have an opening onto the Divine.

Art: Opening onto Transcendence

In a letter that Vincent van Gogh wrote to his brother, Theo, in 1888, he says,

6. Douglas Coupland, *Life after God* (New York: Simon & Schuster/Pocket Books, 1994), pp. 273-74.

I feel more and more that we must not judge of God from this world, it's just a study that didn't come off. . . . This world was evidently slapped together in a hurry on one of [God's] bad days, when the artist didn't know what he was doing or didn't have his wits about him. . . . The study is ruined in so many ways. [But] it is only a master who can make such a blunder, and perhaps that is the best consolation we can have out of it, since in that case we have a right to hope . . . that in some other life we'll see something better than this.[7]

However, it is the searching for "something better than this" in *this* life, some gleanings of divinity in the midst of and through the messiness of this world's life, some imagining of a better, more hope-filled world than our current one, that has driven poets and others artists throughout history.

Artistic Works as Religious Acts

Van Gogh, like Coleridge and others before him, saw art as created by human hands, but not by human hands alone. He saw a divine source of imaginative inspiration welling up within artists' souls, "a certain dose of inspiration, a ray from on high, that is not in ourselves," that enticed artists into creating "beautiful things."[8]

I would argue along with others that this romantic view of the creative act is not dead, not by a long shot. Not only is there a religious hunger abroad in the land, but artists themselves tend to view their artistic creations as inspired in some sense by a divine spirit or their own human spirit, creating some meaning never expressed in the same way before their imaginative act — "wrest[ing] meaning from the darkness."[9]

In an essay entitled "A Poet's View," Denise Levertov talks about inspiration or, if you will, *intuition*. For the artist, she says, to believe in inspiration is to know that "without [inspired] Imagination . . . no amount of acquired craft or scholarship or of brilliant reasoning will

---

7. Quoted in Cliff Edwards, *Van Gogh and God* (Chicago: Loyola University Press, 1989), pp. 70-72.

8. Quoted in Edwards, *Van Gogh and God,* p. 76.

9. George Steiner, *Real Presences* (Chicago: University of Chicago Press, 1989), p. 204.

suffice." To believe in inspiration is "to live with a door of one's life open to the transcendent, the numinous."[10]

Along with Coleridge and Levertov, as well as a host of other artists throughout history, I view the imagination's engagement and its aesthetic works as fundamentally religious acts. As I said in the introduction, through our God-given capacity to "read symbols" carrying glints of transcendent truth, we glimpse traces of the God who comes to us. And through our imaginative power to glimpse such truth, we create and co-create through symbols (gestures, metaphoric poems, music, painting, and story) new worlds of meaning, running to meet God in the process.

Thus, by paying close attention, the creative artist perceives symbols of divinity revealed in our own everyday world. And through that imaginative power, the artist — and for Coleridge, pre-eminently the poet — mimics divine creativity in reassembling images and symbols into expressions of truth ultimately divine in origin.

Again, we are all partakers of this divine reality. According to George Steiner and others, we participate in the divine real Presence either as primary creators of artworks or as those who engage deeply with art as well as with ritual and story in our everyday lives. Whether we are making an art object or viewing one, our creative, imaginative involvement with the work is present. According to Robert Barth, "Imagination alone enables us — not just the poet but all of us — to 'hold fit converse with the spiritual world.' [The Imagination] is the 'feeding source' not only for the poet but for us all."[11]

Memory and the Creative Imagination

How does the imagination work in creating an artistic product such as a poem or a painting? How do readers' or viewers' imaginations engage with such a creation to experience some new insight into the truth of their lives, experiencing some transcendent revelation in the process?

10. Denise Levertov, "A Poet's View," in *New and Selected Essays* (New York: New Directions, 1992), p. 241.

11. Robert Barth, *Romanticism and Transcendence* (Columbia: University of Missouri Press, 2003), p. 71.

It seems to me that we are talking about two sorts of truths here. One truth is our human truth, the truth that makes sense, echoing our deepest grasp of lived meaning within the context of our lives. The other truth is God's truth, a divine, transcendent truth that we catch sight of shining through the everyday, revealed by that Symbol Giver in the poetics of the world around us. The gateway of our imagination is the place of intersection between these human and divine realities.

In terms of human truth, I pointed out in our discussion of ritual that what you see or hear would make no sense if it didn't somehow fit with your memory of stored experience. A ritualistic movement or a poetic metaphor wouldn't "speak" to you if it didn't somehow connect in a meaningful way with what you already know of your everyday world. It is this background of personal experience within a shared cultural world of meaning that also provides a fund of images, symbols that the imagination can then reshape into new forms.

Robin Jensen says that "this is the imagination's work — to begin with the familiar as a starting point, and then to focus, shape, twist, or even explode it into something new — yet perhaps keeping enough of the truth of the original so that others might find their experience there too."[12] She goes on to say that it's this recognition of the familiar in the newly created artwork that can stop someone dead in their tracks while hearing a poem recited or viewing a painting, calling forth an exclamation of "That's it! That's exactly my experience! I can resonate with that!"

The artist thus makes connections between his or her own background fund of stored images, and with skill and artistry creates and "bodies forth" aesthetic works to be seen, heard, or touched by others, who in turn recognize some felt truth in those works, something true to their own experience that creates a resonance in their own lives.

However, good art — poetic or visual — has to pierce beneath the mundane, the everyday, and explore the hidden truth beneath what is popular and assumed. Otherwise, the art is merely banal. But this creative process is also a risky one for the artist. When the poet, for example, opens up some human truth that lies beneath the everyday norm by imaginatively re-viewing and re-ordering the world around us, he or

---

12. Robin Jensen, *The Substance of Things Seen* (Grand Rapids: William B. Eerdmans, 2004), p. 16.

she then runs a risk that hearers or viewers of the work won't "get" the symbolic or metaphorical opening up of their taken-for-granted reality. Such mental "gaps" — created by the artist's pushing metaphor or symbol into novel realms of meaning — can be flooded with new meaning only if the viewers or hearers are able to engage with the art object and are open to the questions thus raised.

And that new meaning can open onto divine truth when the imagination of the artist touches the truth of transcendent Mystery with a word or a brush or a chisel, and we as hearers or viewers are truly and imaginatively open to engaging with such mystery. As co-creators we are able to push back the darkness a little by venturing into that yet unseen or unknown, meeting God in the process. And it is to that great mystery and its revelation through art forms that we now turn.

Poetry and Visual Art: Symbol and Story

The encounter with transcendent Mystery through poetry, as through all art forms, can be expressed through abstract symbol or through more fully developed narrative form. Thus there are poems and paintings that convey a more abstract, mystical sense of mystery (leaving a lot to readers' and viewers' imaginations), and there are poems and visual artworks that have a metaphoric tale to tell. We'll look at both forms in the pages ahead.

I want first to turn to Coleridge as an exemplar par excellence of the earlier Romantics' celebration of imaginative power as our human opening onto Transcendence. His understanding of the central role the imagination plays in meeting the Divine provides a background against which to view contemporary poets like Denise Levertov and their creative works.[13]

As we have seen, Coleridge links the imagination as a whole with the human soul and the existence of God as supreme Symbol Giver. The human imagination is also the source of creativity in the arts, and is

---

13. My focus in this chapter is on contemporary poetry. However, I should also point out that Scripture is filled with beautiful poems, even of a mystical variety. Perhaps the best example of this mystical poetry is found in the Song of Songs (or Song of Solomon) in the Hebrew Bible.

most genuinely expressed in poetry. In Coleridge's *Biographia,*[14] the relationship between God and creative imagination "reverberates with the conception of soul,"[15] and Coleridge claims that imaginative creativity expressed in poetry bears witness to our human nature as being created in the divine image.

One of Coleridge's most mystical and exotic poems — which many schoolchildren surely still read (at least in part) at some point in their educational career — is "Kubla Khan." It, along with his "Christabel" and "The Rime of the Ancient Mariner" (a tale told in poetic form), is a prime example of the creative imagination at work — that power to retrieve elements from stored memory and shape them into something familiar but now new, generating novel images, metaphors, and concepts in the process.

Thomas McFarland describes these three particular poems of Coleridge as examples of what he terms created "heterocosms," worlds "parallel to but not found in the brazen world of actuality."[16] In fact, in "Kubla Kahn" we glimpse a visionary world symbolizing fallen man's longing for a lost Eden, and by extension, we see the poetic genius who struggles for paradisaical wholeness despite human flaws.

When Coleridge published "Kubla Kahn" in 1816, he prefaced it with a note that he was publishing this "fragment" of poetry at the behest of Lord Byron. He added that he was publishing it not because it had any particular poetic merit, but because it was a "psychological curiosity," since he had written it in a trance-like state.

Apparently Coleridge at that time was quite fascinated with the creative process itself, and the role that the inspired imagination and unconscious mechanisms might play in it. As Richard Holmes puts it, Coleridge's fragments of poetry, here and in other works of his, "bring us as close as we can get to the threshold of the creative process itself."[17]

In his preface to the poem, Coleridge explains that he had been ill

14. Samuel Taylor Coleridge, *Biographia Literaria, or Biographical Sketches of My Literary Life and Opinions,* ed. James Engell and W. Jackson Bate (Princeton: Princeton University Press, 1983).

15. Thomas McFarland, *Originality and Imagination* (Baltimore: Johns Hopkins University Press, 1985), p. 122.

16. McFarland, *Originality and Imagination,* p. 123.

17. Richard Holmes, in *Samuel Taylor Coleridge: Selected Poems,* ed. Richard Holmes (New York: Penguin Books, 1994), p. 226.

at the time and had retired to a country house where he had been pre-
scribed an "anodyne" that caused him to sleep. And during sleep, his
creative mind had composed a long poem, two or three hundred lines
in length, the poetic unconscious being accessible in a "sort of reverie."
Upon waking, he attempted to re-create the work, but was called away
and thus interrupted in the process. When he returned to continue his
attempt, he found that most of the poem had faded from memory "like
the images on the surface of a stream into which a stone has been cast."
This "fragment" preserved all that he could remember of it.[18]

Of course, there's no way of knowing if Coleridge's mind did com-
pose hundreds of lines of poetry while he was in a trance-like doze. But
as Holmes notes, the reader of the poem does have the sense that there
is a greater whole into which the fragment fits. This fragment of the
whole conveys a sense of Paradise lost, of fallen man and that lost Garden, where the now-flawed human tries to rebuild that world which is
now gone.

Finally, Coleridge "dreams" of such a paradise regained, visualizing
a moment of miraculous harmony and wholeness: "It was a miracle of
rare device,/A sunny pleasure-dome with caves of ice!"[19] This vision of
harmony is finally followed by one glimpse of paradise regained:

> That with music loud and long,
> I would build that dome in air,
> That sunny dome! Those caves of ice!
> And all who heard should see them there,
> And all should cry, Beware! Beware!
> His flashing eyes, his floating hair!
> Weave a circle round him thrice,
> And close your eyes with holy dread,
> For he on honey-dew hath fed
> And drunk the milk of Paradise.[20]

In commenting on the poem, John Beer says, "The bare anatomy of
meaning is covered by a clothing of exotic language, glimmering and

---

18. John Beer, in *S. T. Coleridge: Poems,* Everyman's Library edition, ed. John Beer
(New York: Alfred A. Knopf, 1991), pp. 163-64.

19. "Kubla Khan," stanza 3, lines 15-16.

20. "Kubla Khan," stanza 4, lines 9-18.

glittering by turns. The various appeals to the senses in ice and moon-light . . . paradise milk and paradise honey are skillfully deployed. Crystalline and drowsy by turns, the poem, as a verbal structure, exists in a total mood of dreamy enchantment."[21]

As his entire body of poetic work suggests, Coleridge was apparently enthralled with the relationship between images of physical light and the "inward illumination" of poetic, imaginative inspiration, both in physical actuality and in meaningful metaphor. For him the symbol remained the "translucence of the eternal through and in the temporal."[22] God speaks to the soul through the imagination and its artistic products.

Modern and Postmodern Glimpses of God through Poetry

Although Coleridge became increasingly orthodox in his religious beliefs as he aged, the Romantic movement of which he was a part saw the source of revelation apart from traditional religious sources such as Scripture. The artist's creative imagination, under the influence of divine inspiration, revealed traces of divinity within nature, refashioned principally by that imagination.

As I indicated at the beginning of this chapter, and as Peggy Rosenthal underscored, Romanticism's attack on authoritarian religious structures as repressive to individual freedom, along with questions regarding traditional interpretations of Scripture raised within the religious establishment itself, shook the foundations of religious certitude. Additionally, the disillusionment resulting from industrialization and its social effects, as well as the horrors of modern warfare, left in their wake only shredded structures of meaning. Within literary circles and even among the population at large, people were left bewildered.

Thus, contemporary poets and other artists speak for the human condition as they find it and live it, struggling to discover some spark of inspired truth beneath the surface of our disenchanted technological

---

21. Beer, in *S. T. Coleridge: Poems*, p. 166.

22. Samuel Taylor Coleridge, *The Statesman's Manual*, in *Lay Sermons*, ed. R. J. White, vol. 6 of *The Collected Works of Samuel Taylor Coleridge*, ed. Katherine Coburn (Princeton: Princeton University Press, 1972), p. 30.

world, a spark of "paradoxical light" in the darkness.[23] Through their various imaginative artworks, a number of contemporary poets and other artists seek to create some symbolic hint of Transcendence, evoking some sense of a veiled reality beyond the everyday.

In this section I have chosen to look at selected works of four poets: R. S. Thomas, Wendell Berry, Denise Levertov, and W. H. Auden. I have chosen them because they represent what I believe is among the best in modern/postmodern poetry. In their work I find a struggle for faith in the midst of anguishing doubts and questions, a hope in a transcendent Presence, and the creation of images in metaphoric language that evokes a sense of the holy in the reader.

R. S. Thomas: Waiting in the Silence

In the "melancholy, withdrawing roar" of God's waning presence in the modern world, writers and other artists have sometimes celebrated human freedom from religious restraint, but more often have lamented the sense of God's absence and thus the erosion of any sense of ultimate meaning from our lives. Beckett's *Waiting for Godot* is indeed a bleak testimony to this long and perhaps futile wait for some answer, some redemption from this life of solitary suffering. Even if one suffers with others, one finally is alone on a stage empty of any ultimate meaning.

But other artists ask questions. "Why is God silent?" "What does it mean to be human?" "Why is there horrendous, innocent suffering in the face of inexplicable evil?" "Where is God in all of this?" And some ask the questions addressed to divine or transcendent Mystery with a tenacious clinging to hope, some sense that there is a Listener who undergirds all of life.

R. S. Thomas is one of this second group writing within an ultimate framework of faith. Many of his poems are about the long wait of George Steiner's Saturday metaphor — waiting in prayer, waiting in church, waiting for some sign from the wholly Other that human existence ultimately makes sense. Born in 1913, Thomas is an Anglican priest in the Church of Wales. He has spent his entire adult life being faithful to his priestly calling, and he has also written a large number of

---

23. Paul Mariani, "The Ineffability of What Counts," in his *God and the Imagination* (Athens: University of Georgia Press, 2002), p. 231.

poems "circling around the core of God's utter silence."[24] Here is the voice of this poet in "Via Negativa," which he wrote in 1972:

> Why no! I never thought other than
> That God is that great absence
> In our lives, the empty silence
> Within, the place where we go
> Seeking, not in hope to
> Arrive or find. He keeps the interstices
> In our knowledge, the darkness
> Between stars. His are the echoes
> We follow, the footprints he has just
> Left. We put our hands in
> His side hoping to find
> It warm. We look at people
> And places as though he had looked
> At them, too; but miss the reflection.[25]

The very title of this often-quoted poem reflects the mystical tradition known as the apophatic tradition, the grasping after ultimate mystery — the no-thingness of the wholly Other — by way of nothingness, by letting go of all visible, material form to seek the God behind all created forms. Thomas seeks God in the silence, in absence, paradoxically seeking out God in language and image, since this is the only access we have to the Divine. Indeed, Thomas's entire poetic career is shot through with what Peggy Rosenthal calls "this tension between needing to use words as his medium and distrusting their capacity to mediate what truly matters."[26] Yet traces of God haunt our consciousness, while divine mystery itself, "darkness between stars," transcends our world.

Another image found in many of Thomas's poems is the biblical symbol of the "doubting" Thomas in John's Gospel. Placing his hand in the side of Jesus' wound, Thomas hopes there to "find it warm," hopes to find some sense of incarnate, touchable concreteness to God's presence still with us. Again, story and image together convey meaning,

---

24. Rosenthal, *The Poets' Jesus*, p. 127.

25. "Via Negativa," in *The Poems of R. S. Thomas* (Fayetteville: University of Arkansas Press, 1985), p. 75.

26. Rosenthal, *The Poets' Jesus*, p. 130.

since in order to appreciate the "wound" symbol within these poems, the reader clearly needs to know the Gospel story. Rosenthal comments on this image of the gaping hole: "It seems grotesque . . . to be imaginatively inside a gaping wound. Yet what a powerful image for the cosmic pain and emptiness at the center of human existence . . . making the hole in his side the site of our search for 'that great absence/In our lives' that is God."[27]

In many of Thomas's poems, the reader gets the sense of this faithful priest sitting in a darkened church, waiting for some sign, waiting for God's word to be heard. In "The Empty Church," Thomas likens his prayers to matches, striking God's silent, stony heart. He asks,

> . . . Why, then, do I kneel still
> striking my prayers on a stone
> heart? Is it in hope one
> of them will ignite yet and throw
> on its illumined walls the shadow
> of someone greater than I can understand?[28]

And at the end of another poem titled simply "Kneeling," Thomas says, ". . . When I speak,/Though it be you who speak/Through me, something is lost./The meaning is in the waiting."[29]

The meaning is in the waiting — this theme cuts across the works of Eliot, Auden, Levertov, and many other artists of our day. But the essential difference between the waiting in Beckett's *Waiting for Godot* and the waiting expressed in Thomas's work and that of other contemporary religious poets is that, as Rosenthal notes, Beckett waits out the day in a secular century's doubt and emptiness; Thomas and others of his company wait in a faith "ripened" by two thousand years of tradition.

Perhaps Thomas's poems can give something to those who teeter between the worlds of Beckett and Thomas, can provide, as Jill Baumgaertner suggests, "a unique angle of vision for those whose imaginations have atrophied." She asks, "How can we know anything

---

27. Rosenthal, *The Poets' Jesus,* pp. 130-31.

28. "The Empty Church" (stanza 2, lines 1-6), in *The Poems of R. S. Thomas,* pp. 122-23.

29. "Kneeling" (stanza 2, lines 2-5), in *The Poems of R. S. Thomas,* p. 61.

of God if our senses have not been trained and our imagination is dead?"[30] For it is in the imagination that faith begins because we cannot see the face of God. To engage deeply with the poetry of R. S. Thomas is to open up one's imagination to the presence of an ineffable Other.

Wendell Berry: Glimpsing God in Nature

Berry (born in 1934), a Kentucky farmer for forty years, a poet and an essayist, is a writer whose imagination is grounded in the land of his region. In homely images of family and friends, bridles and barns, pasture and woods, local fields and community, he — along with writers such as William Carlos Williams — penetrates the depths of the local and the everyday to uncover glimpses of God.

In one of Berry's most self-consciously religious verses — in my view almost a perfect poem — he writes,

> We travelers, walking to the sun, can't see
> Ahead, but looking back the very light
> That blinded us shows us the way we came,
> Along which blessings now appear, risen
> As if from sightlessness to sight, and we,
> By blessing brightly lit, keep going toward
> That blessed light that yet to us is dark.[31]

I have read and reread this poem many times, and each time the reading is a blessing. The brilliance of God's light blinds us on our journey toward him. It is only as we look back over the journey — lit by God's light from behind us as we turn — that we can see the blessings along the way, "risen as if from sightlessness to sight." And it is these blessings that we've received in our journey along the way that now light our path as we continue to travel toward that blinding, eternal Light.

This poem is among his collection of works simply titled "Sabbath

30. Jill Palaez Baumgaertner, "Hints of Redemption," *Christian Century,* 21 February 2006, p. 42.

31. Wendell Berry, "We travelers, walking to the sun," in *Given: New Poems* (Emeryville, Calif.: Shoemaker Hoard, an imprint of Avalon Publishing Group, Inc., 2005), p. 74.

Poems." In another poem from this same collection, symbols of death and transformation shine through the images:

> We come at last to the dark
> and enter in. We are given bodies
> newly made out of their absence
> from one another in the light
> of the ordinary day. We come
> to the space between ourselves,
> the narrow doorway, and pass through
> into the land of the wholly loved.[32]

Coming at last to the dark of death and crossing that threshold, we are given resurrected and transformed bodies — bodies that we normally can't see in the ordinary light of the everyday. The image of the "narrow doorway" has a biblical echo to it, recalling the perhaps familiar Gospel passage where Jesus refers to the narrow "door" to eternal life. And when we pass through that door, we enter into "the land of the wholly loved," the land where God who is Love welcomes the traveler home.

Of course, each of you reading these poems may have a different take on their meaning. Out of your own experience, out of your own background and personality, your imaginative engagement — your co-creation with Berry and the other poets explored here — you may very well produce different images and different meanings in the process. But with the "angle of vision" given by the poet's language, through the sensuous images and fragments of scripture, through sound effects and rhythm, through the odd juxtaposing of jarring metaphors, the transcendent meaning beneath the everyday world can shine through the artist's imaginative creation.

Denise Levertov: Poetry of Faith

Denise Levertov's life as a writer spanned most of the twentieth century: she was born in 1923 and died in 1997. Her mother, who was Welsh, was a Christian; her father, who was Russian, was a Hasidic Jew who later converted to Christianity and became an Anglican priest. In 1948 she moved to the United States, where she subsequently became a

---

32. Berry, "We come at last to the dark," in *Given,* p. 107.

well-known poet. Never quite fitting into either a Jewish or a Christian world, never quite feeling at home in either England or the States, Levertov apparently lived comfortably on the margins of these societies, where she could critically view the social and cultural movements of the times. Influenced by the writings of Rainer Maria Rilke and William Carlos Williams, she also explored the mystery in the everyday world around us.

Her life as a poet took on the shape of a religious pilgrimage; she says she moved from "regretful skepticism" to Christian belief by the vehicle of her work, which "enfaithed" her. Levertov came to see the imagination as able to penetrate the depths of human and divine truth. And following the road of the imagination, her work as a poet ". . . risk[ed] the abyss . . . endure[d] the cloud of unknowing . . . yield[ed] itself to fiery light."[33]

In an essay about her work and her faith journey, Levertov links her life as a poet with her deepening religious faith. Like Coleridge before her, she asserts a belief in the "truth of the imagination," likening her following of her intuition and imaginative inspiration to what Quakers refer to as "following a leading," which means being open to and speaking out of the promptings of the Spirit. In a sense, every work of art — poem, painting, or sculpture — is an "act of faith," a "venturing out into the mystery of the unknown."[34]

Like Wendell Berry, Levertov frequently uses images drawn from nature to express something of the Divine. In a poem titled "In Whom We Live and Move and Have Our Being," she employs the flight of birds as a metaphor for our riding on God's spirit as the undergirding current in our lives:

> Birds afloat in airs current,
> sacred breath? No, not breath of God,
> it seems, but God
> the air enveloping the whole
> globe of being.
> It's we who breathe, in, out, in, the sacred,

33. Denise Levertov, *New and Selected Essays* (New York: New Directions, 1992), p. 41.

34. Levertov, quoted in Rosenthal, *The Poets' Jesus*, p. 170. For a further elaboration on this theme, see also Mariani's work, *God and the Imagination*, pp. 233-44.

leaves astir, our wings
rising, ruffled — but only the saints
take flight. We cower
in cliff-crevice or edge out gingerly
on branches close to the nest . . .
But storm or still,
numb or poised in attention,
We inhale, exhale, inhale,
encompassed, encompassed.[35]

Whether we take off in flight or cling to our branch, our wings, our thoughts, our imaginations, our senses are stirred and sustained by God's spirit. We breathe in the divine Presence that upholds our being, we "in-spire" God's spirit, which encompasses us in our daily lives, whether or not we have the courage of saints to sail out into the unknown abyss.

Some of Levertov's poems are more explicitly Christian in content, and some, like one she titled "The Annunciation," have a stronger narrative shape. But I think the one given here is fairly representative of her poems in its expression of wonder at the awesome presence of the Transcendent in our daily lives.

The poetry we have considered up until now I have called "mystical" in the sense that these poems likely evoke a sense of God's presence outside of a framework of narrative or story. However, it is a basic premise of this book that our consciousness — whether awake or asleep — has an inherently narrative shape to it. As I discussed earlier, humans have an essential tendency to tell stories, to think and dream in temporal terms, first a "this" and then a "that." So I would argue that you as reader likely supplied some kind of story of your own in the reading of the mystical poetry in which we have just immersed ourselves, even though the narrative shape was mostly ambiguous and hidden.

For example, in reading that first poem by Berry ("We travelers, walking to the sun . . .") and Thomas's poems about waiting ("Why, then, do I kneel still . . ."), I supplied my own story, thinking back on

---

35. Denise Levertov, "In Whom We Live and Move and Have Our Being," in *Denise Levertov: Selected Poems*, ed. Paul Lacey (New York: New Directions, 2002), p. 194.

the blessings of my life or remembering the times of waiting for a sign from God in the church, and then what might come next. In a sense, I co-created the meaning of the poems, shaping narratives in the process.

W. H. Auden: Anxiety before Transcendent Mystery

The Auden poem that I quote here is an example of poetic expression as story.[36] In fact, there are long sections within the poem that are nearly pure narrative. Auden, along with T. S. Eliot and others, struggled with the gap between our human, limited knowing and God's reality. As a consequence, he fills his poems with images of both secular and religious anxiety, as well as with metaphoric symbols of doubt that faith somehow has to face. Auden not only reflects on the human void left by a sense of God's absence, but he also imaginatively addresses, through parody and satire, the political, social, and amoral (as well as immoral) mid-twentieth-century scene, which distracted and seduced people away from attending to what really matters.

"For the Time Being: A Christmas Oratorio" was composed between 1941 and 1942, and in it Auden juxtaposes the Gospel story of Jesus' birth and the European world just prior to World War II.[37] Written and dedicated to his mother, who had just died, the poem is one of the few unambiguously religious works that Auden created. In it he uses a variety of forms, including lengthy, sometimes quite witty sections of prose poetry, much of it reflecting keen psychological insight into the flaws and foibles of human nature.

This long poem is divided into nine parts, the first titled "Advent," which opens with rhythmic choral passages. The various parts follow the course of the Nativity story, from the Annunciation to Mary by the angel Gabriel; to scenes of the wise men, the shepherds, and the manger; to the final massacre of the Innocents. Although it is too long to quote in its entirety here, I've chosen some excerpts to show how Auden imaginatively opens up both a sense of secular estrangement from God — who is still present in *our* absence — and a sense of belea-

---

36. In this section on Auden I am indebted to Anthony Hecht's volume entitled *The Hidden Law: The Poetry of W. H. Auden* (Cambridge: Harvard University Press, 1993).

37. W. H. Auden, "For the Time Being," in *Collected Longer Poems* (New York: Random House, 2002), pp. 131-98.

guered belief for — as Anthony Hecht puts it — those odd enough still to embrace religious faith in a time such as ours.[38]

Early on in the poem, the figure of the narrator, speaking in prose poetry, shifts back and forth between a satirical focusing on society in the voice of an officious bureaucrat ("These are stirring times for the editors of newspapers:/History is in the making; Mankind is on the march")[39] and a reflection on our contemporary condition of distraction away from the Transcendent: "If we were never alone or always too busy,/Perhaps we might even believe what we know is not true:/ But no one is taken in, at least not all of the time;/In our bath, or the subway, or the middle of the night,/We know very well we are not unlucky but evil,/that the dream of a Perfect State or No State at all,/To which we fly for refuge, is a part of our punishment."[40] It is when we are alone with ourselves that we must confront our naive delusions about our political arrangements, as well as certain truths about our public lives that our normal busyness tends to mask.

At the close of this work, the narrator again pulls us away from the struggles of the Holy Family to our own struggles as we live out our distracted daily lives. Shining a light on our contemporary scene, the prose poem illumines our yearly, dreary clean-up after Christmas festivities, when we pack away the ornaments and soberly head back to our daily rounds in the "real world."

> Well, so that is that. Now we must dismantle the tree,
> Putting the decorations back into their cardboard boxes —
> Some have got broken — and carrying them up into the attic.[41]

As Hecht observes, after the holidays the naive and happy illusions of childhood are also packed away, and we are returned to the world of doubters, the world of work deadlines and closet clutter. And those marginal few who cling to the faith in the wake of fading Christmas joy must face the long, sad trek to Lent and to that Friday that some call Good.

---

38. Hecht, *The Hidden Law*, p. 291.
39. Auden, "For the Time Being," Part 4, section IV, lines 1-2.
40. Auden, "For the Time Being," Part 4, section IV, lines 18-24.
41. Auden, "For the Time Being," Part 9, section III, lines 1-3.

The happy morning is over,
The night of agony still to come; the time is noon:
When the Spirit must practice his scales of rejoicing
Without even a hostile audience, and the Soul endure
A silence that is neither for nor against her faith
That God's Will will be done. . . .[42]

The time is noon, or Steiner's and McEwan's Saturday, that time in between, that time for the time being, that time in which we live and struggle in our journeys of doubt and feeble faith. Auden seems to say that all those who opt for Pascal's wager that God is and that God waits for each of us — all those with such faith travel in an alien land for the time being.

Visual Symbol and Story: Meeting God in Paintings and Sculpture

Robin Jensen makes a strong argument for the power of pictures *over* words. She says that what we see, sometimes even in passing, becomes what we are, becomes unshakable from memory. I think we can all remember vividly certain images — snapshots, films, journalistic photos — that have become indelibly imprinted on our brains.[43]

For me it is an image that appeared on the front page of a newspaper during the Gulf War period. The picture showed a line of our troops, kneeling as if in prayer, with gas masks completely covering their faces. They looked something like muzzled dogs, staring into the camera. It was a startling juxtaposition of the horrors of biological warfare and the posture of prayer. Images can have a searing effect, while words fade from memory.

Yet while Jensen says that "words can never adequately describe what we see and know through that process of seeing,"[44] she nevertheless insists that images — even perhaps the most abstract, symbolic works of art — cannot be completely detached from the metaphors and stories of our tradition. As she explains, "The meaning of pictures depends on the

42. Auden, "For the Time Being," Part 9, section III, lines 47-52.
43. Jensen, *The Substance of Things Seen.*
44. Jensen, *The Substance of Things Seen*, p. 48.

interactivity with the stories and the familiar interpretations of those stories as known to the observers . . . and . . . finally by the imagination and
insight of the viewers themselves."[45] Again, the engaged viewer thus becomes a co-creator with the artist, responding out of her own tradition
and history, using her own imagination to create a story for herself.

For example, I have just come across a painting by the Dutch artist
Jan Vanriet entitled *Three Nails*. It's a 13 × 8½″ watercolor depicting
three large, spiky black nails painted on a mostly blood-red background.
If you are a product of Western Christian culture, it is a startling image
suggesting the Crucifixion — with "no body, no blood, no wounds, no
crown of thorns — just nails in wood. The suffering — crucified one — is
absent but fully present. There is something fearful about it."[46] It is a very
evocative piece, and finally deeply meaningful if you know the story of
the Crucifixion as a symbol of ultimate hope beyond evil and suffering.

Good paintings, like all good art, say something true — about the
human condition, about life, about the mystery at the core of life. Good
art speaks something true beyond words, opening up the unseen
through visual display; it has the power to startle us, the power to force
us to struggle with what we really believe about what matters beneath
the surface of things. This is all true, whether the subject matter is self-
consciously "religious" or not.

There is such an incredible wealth of good visual art we could focus
on here — for example, Picasso's *Guernica,* Edvard Munch's *The
Scream,* Chagall's *Moses Receiving the Tablets of the Law* — just as there
are so many good poems and stories we could use as illustrative examples for the purposes of this book. But I have chosen a still life by Van
Gogh because, besides being relatively easy for the reader to visualize,
its symbolic meaning is imaginatively fleshed out by the viewer's
knowledge of the stories behind the images.

Van Gogh's Still Life with Open Bible and Zola Novel

Vincent van Gogh painted the work *Still Life with Open Bible and Zola
Novel* in 1885. As the title of the work suggests, he painted a table on

---

45. Jensen, *The Substance of Things Seen,* p. 50.
46. "A Conversation with Godfried Cardinal Danneels," *Image* 54 (Summer 2007):
33-34.

which a Bible rests (his father's, it turns out), along with a candlestick holding the stub of an extinguished candle, and a worn paperback novel by Émile Zola, *La Joie de Vivre (The Joy of Living)*. The Bible is open to Isaiah 53.

If you know Zola's novel (the story of a young girl who joyfully embraces the raising of an infant in the midst of desolation, a "light shining in the darkness"), and if you know that the writer of Second Isaiah (chapters 40–55) was a prophet of hope for the future, then through the blending power of your imagination, you'll appreciate the meaning of the work more deeply than if you saw it merely as a dark and somewhat complex still life.

But as Cliff Edwards points out, Van Gogh was apparently saying something else through the images displayed on the canvas. Through the Bible, candle, and novel, Van Gogh was also saying something about the glint of truth that can be seen within secular works of art. God's revelation speaks powerfully to our imaginations from the pages of a novel such as Zola's — perhaps sometimes more clearly than prophetic Scripture does.[47]

As I said earlier, word and image, story and picture go together to create meaning. As Jensen puts it, "Words can never adequately describe what we see and know through the process of seeing, nor can images be completely detached from ideas or language or — most of all — stories. They both lead to a fuller, richer apprehension of an idea."[48]

Lynn Aldrich's Paper-Plate Columns

As the book of Genesis has it, God created Adam out of the dust of the earth and pronounced his creation as good. So God as Divine Sculptor created human form. And humans have been sculpting ever since! From the most ancient of times, humans have stacked stone upon stone to make an altar, have fashioned their carvings into likenesses of their gods. "Through the centuries," Lynn Aldrich points out, "sculpture has

---

47. See Cliff Edwards' *Van Gogh and God* (Chicago: Loyola University Press, 1989), for an extensive discussion of this and other works of Van Gogh and their religious significance.

48. Jensen, *The Substance of Things Seen*, p. 48.

continued to serve the role of marker, memorial, and monument," lending it "an air of awesome immobility or permanence."[49]

More recently, as the spirit of modernism and postmodernism has swept through the arts, sculpted pieces have also become more abstract in form, drawing the viewer's contribution into the creative process. This way of negativity, reflecting the final unknowability of God and the search for hints of Transcendence within the limits of language, image, and the material world around us, is a path common to many modern/postmodern artists.

Aldrich is a contemporary sculptor who lives and works in Los Angeles. To provide an example of contemporary abstract art meant to express symbolic, transcendent meaning, she writes about one of her own sculptures entitled *Western Civ.* (1995), on display in an art gallery in Venice, California. She describes her artistic method: She begins by observing simple, banal objects around her and then incorporating them, imaginatively working with the material, to express aesthetically her experience of human truth and Transcendence.

She created this particular piece by stacking ten-foot-tall columns of paper plates that lean precariously into a corner of the display, held in place "miraculously" only by gravity. She comments,

> It is a beautiful and silly, white, Grecian column. . . . In a way, this work is a critique of the very idea of stability or permanence; it has an inept monumentality which I associate with what it is to be human, paradoxically flawed yet "in God's image." . . . I construct each work while imagining that its final form will somehow hint or whisper at the visitation of God into his creation.[50]

Aldrich's method of observation and her working with the inner properties of the "stuff" she finds in her environment — including pine needles, cacti, insect bodies, paper plates, fake fur, and plastic roofing material — involve an imaginative process of attention to the world around her, an engagement, she says, with the inner character of her materials, their reality.

---

49. Lynn Aldrich, "What's the Matter with Matter?" in *Beholding the Glory: Incarnation through the Arts,* ed. Jeremy Begbie (Grand Rapids: Baker Academic, 2001), pp. 106-7.
50. Aldrich, "What's the Matter with Matter?" p. 115.

*　　*　　*

The poet Rilke refers to our imagination's glimpse of reality beneath the surface of the everyday, that revelatory seeing, as "inseeing," really looking beneath the visible surface of things to imagine their core essence or meaning. I think that all of the artistic examples explored here capture that deep impression things make, from Thomas's silent church that speaks of the silence of God to Aldrich's paper-plate columns that convey creation's God-haunted, precarious majesty — they offer "shafts of epiphany in the gloomy grind of the mundane."[51]

World Projection in Poetry and Art:
The Responsibility of Artist and Audience

If, as I have affirmed in these pages, the imagination is key to our perception of reality and thus to our openness to God, then it follows that those who shape the imagination through their artwork have a grave responsibility for the worlds of meaning they create and project. This is true because the imagination opens out onto evil as well as good, and the creation of meaning between giver and receiver is for good or for ill. Just as we are what we eat, just as we become who we are in relationship with one another, so we become what we see and what we read.

Thus, I think there is a corollary imperative for us to become responsible consumers of art as we choose in our freedom the poems we read, the movies we watch, the paintings and photographs we gaze at in gallery and studio. Here we will look first at the responsibility of the artist before turning to the co-creative responsibility of those who engage art in all its forms.

George Steiner says that no serious writer, painter, or composer has ever doubted that his or her work bears on good and evil, "on the enhancement or diminution of the sum of humanity in man and the city":

A message is being sent; to a purpose. The style, the explicit figurations of that message may be perverse, they may intend the subjuga-

---

51. Andrew Rumsey, "Through Poetry: Particularity and the Call to Attention," in Begbie, *Beholding the Glory,* p. 55.

tion, even the ruin of the recipient. They may claim for themselves, as in Sade, as in the black paintings of Goya, as in the death-dance of Artaud, the somber license of the suicidal. But their pertinence to questions and consequences of an ethical order is the more palpable. Only trash, only *kitsch* and . . . music which are produced solely for monetary or propagandistic ends do, indeed, transcend . . . morality. Theirs is the pornography of insignificance.[52]

Again, if art projects a world of meaning, and images taken up and reassembled by our imaginations have the power to sear our brains and shape our perception of reality — if aesthetic forms in music, poetry, and paintings have such persuasive conscious and even unconscious force — then the questions of *purpose* enter into the discussion.

The Responsibility of the Artist

The first time I saw a print of Matthias Grünewald's fifteenth-century Isenheim Altarpiece, which depicts the Crucifixion, I was mesmerized by it — and appalled by it. The gaunt, torn body of Christ gruesomely hangs from nails, his head sunk against his chest, his fingers tortuously "splayed as if in a last entreaty for release from pain."[53]

The altarpiece was commissioned by a religious order that cared for those suffering from a fatal bacterial disease called St. Anthony's fire, and the body of Christ, as well as one of the other figures in the painting, is covered with loathsome sores most likely resembling the effects of that disease. Thus, Grünewald's altarpiece symbolically creates an almost overwhelming vision of human suffering. But it also portrays the divine Christ suffering along with the dying patients who must have gazed at the painting daily.[54]

Truly, sometimes the images that art portrays are shocking. In fact, artworks throughout history — the paintings of Caravaggio, Botticelli, Van Gogh, Picasso, and Rouault in their own time, the poems of Blake and Whitman — have stirred as well as shocked the imaginations of both the church and the public. As Robin Jensen points out, today we

52. Steiner, *Real Presences,* p. 145.
53. Jensen, *The Substance of Things Seen,* p. 140.
54. Jensen, *The Substance of Things Seen,* chapter six.

see warning signs attached to particular art exhibits, noting that such contemporary works as *Virgin Mary with Elephant Dung* might offend some viewers. If art's images have always offended some, I think it is important to consider moral parameters and the limits of freedom in those who create.

In her essay "The Poet in the World," Denise Levertov insists that artists have a moral obligation to engage in what is true to their world and important in their time, and that artists are also morally responsible for the *effects* of their work. "When words [and pictures] penetrate deep into us," she says, "they change the chemistry of the soul, of the imagination."[55] Prophetic works such as Picasso's *Guernica* and Mark Twain's long poem "War Prayer," both of which vividly portray the horrors of war, are works that illuminate and expose social evil, reproach the indifferent, and potentially transform the receiver's attitudes and world vision.

Beyond the prophetic, the purposes of art are many — to provide aesthetic delight, to evoke emotion, to communicate knowledge, to enhance worship, and so on. According to Nicholas Wolterstorff, works of art are thus embedded in the fabric of human intention — as Steiner says, for a purpose. Wolterstorff insists that ultimately the purpose of an artist's vocation is to benefit humanity, to praise the Creator, to invite the viewer or listener or reader, through the co-creative power of his or her imagination, to "rejoice with me!" Wolterstorff acknowledges that some modern art can be aesthetically good and at the same time morally bad, and so concludes that ultimately the artist should choose illuminating work that opens up the imagination to a hope-filled future, sacrificing his or her creative pleasure in the possible for its own sake, sacrificing such artistic impulse for the sake of others, for the benefit of the public.[56]

But if "good art" penetrates the often dreary and mundane surface to illumine depths of meaning that challenge our assumptions and open us to new insight and even transcendent vision, then what are we to make of an art photograph created by Andres Serrano that pictures a crucifix submerged in a bucket of blood and urine? Despite the controversy which that artwork caused, Robin Jensen points out that Serrano intended to imaginatively juxtapose the sacred and the profane. She

---

55. Levertov, "The Poet in the World," *New and Selected Essays*, p. 136.

56. Nicholas Wolterstorff, *Art in Action: Toward a Christian Aesthetic* (Grand Rapids: William B. Eerdmans, 1980), p. 4.

sees the work as symbolizing Christ's insertion into the mundane and the sanctification of all of human life. "Like Grünewald's gruesome Christ that is transformed into a radiant, transcendent one, Serrano's crucifix is submerged in what it means to be human, and in that submergence finds a glowing, golden beauty."[57]

In this context, Jensen refers to "primal emotions" that are stirred when viewers perceive sacred symbols being desecrated (recall the uprising in certain quarters of the Muslim world over the cartoon depictions of Muhammad in a Danish newspaper). Clearly, with respect to Serrano's photograph, we witness a clash between the artist's creative intent and what many viewers imaginatively perceive in the work.

Is Serrano's piece "good art"? Does it contribute to the joy and *shalom* of the community? Does it open up a world of transcendent, hope-filled meaning to those who gaze at it? Does it, as Jensen suggests, "inspire the viewer to greater love and compassion for the world in which we live"? She seems to come down on the side of the affirmative in this case. If a work is not intentionally offensive, if it serves the purpose of challenging and provoking questions of deep meaning and struggles of faith in those who look at it, if the sensibilities of the audience are considered, and if the work is displayed or presented in a way that is appropriate to the place and time, then she seems to believe that little is off-limits to the artist.

Perhaps, in the end, weighing the good of the community and the purpose of the message intended by the artist, censorship is not the answer. In the end, maybe all *good* art, a gift of inspiration — lighting up the artist's imagination from some creative Source — exposes the world's flaws and limits, illuminating something better within and beyond this creation.

The Responsibility of the Audience

We have now considered the responsibility of the artist. But what about the responsibility of the audience, those of us who are free to imaginatively engage or not with what is presented? Is there an imperative here that calls each of us to imaginatively engage poetic words that skirt the

57. Jensen, *The Substance of Things Seen,* p. 142.

edges of what can be known, to plumb the depths of what is even grotesquely imaged? Is there an imperative to discern the workings of the Spirit amid even the grimness and messiness of everyday life, to glimpse something true, to uncover and illumine that which really matters?

Toward the end of *Real Presences,* George Steiner speaks of the "courtesy" of the open mind, the willing engagement with literature and art that tells us something important for us to know. "We light the lamp at the window," we respond out of our freedom to imagine and co-create with the artist some truth beneath the appearance of things.[58]

Of course, we are free to close the imagination's gateway, to elect to play bingo or watch "reality TV" instead. Thus we along with Steiner are speaking of two freedoms: the freedom of the artistic giver and the freedom of the responsible receiver, which *together* create a meaning between them. Then, every once in a while, in our openness to another, in our own freedom of response to a work of art, we experience a jolt of recognition, a sense of visitation and summons from without and beyond ourselves, a recognition that seems to occur not by an act of will. Steiner expresses it this way: "The shock of correspondence — it can be muted and nearly indiscernibly gradual — is one of being possessed by that which one comes to possess. . . . We have met before."[59]

Maybe we can end where we began: by asserting that *all* good art — poetry, painting, music, literature, film — creates an opening through the imagination's gateway where, by the grace of God, the mysterious Ineffable shines through. The arts are grounded in the stuff of our lives — in stone, in pigment on canvas, in everyday words of our language that spin symbols and metaphors that break open the mundane. Those artists who speak of things that matter have "pressed on the limits of their own imaginations and . . . have provided a few handholds and footholds to help us to peer across the abyss [of mystery] ourselves."[60] Their imaginative creations and our imaginative engagement with their offerings provide life-giving sustenance for our journey home, giving us hope-filled glimpses of the Transcendent along the way.

58. Steiner, *Real Presences,* p. 149.
59. Steiner, *Real Presences,* p. 180.
60. Christopher Herbert, "Faith and Imagination," *Anglican Theological Review* 87, no. 3 (2005): 396.

CHAPTER THREE

Meeting God in the Story Told:
Sacred and Secular Narratives

Since I have long since come to believe that all of our stories are at their deepest level the same story, it is my hope that in listening to [truly great writers] say so powerfully not what they thought they ought to say, but what they truly felt, we may possibly learn something about how to bear the weight of our own sadness.

Frederick Buechner, *Speak What We Feel*[1]

Our pluralistic contemporary scene is conducive to openness and questioning, freeing many from orthodox dogmas and opening up questions of ultimacy and purpose. For at least some, such freedom from the constraints of orthodoxy has released a quest for spiritual meaning in an age hungry for some kind of transcendent mooring. For others of a more fundamentalist bent, books, films, and plays conveying this sense of openness can be viewed as "dangerous" because they invite multiple interpretations. Whatever the stripe of the seeker, this remains constant: Good stories make us think.

---

1. Frederick Buechner, *Speak What We Feel* (San Francisco: HarperSanFrancisco, 2001), p. xi.

74

The Transformative Power of Storytelling

Each of us has our own tale to tell, since telling stories seems to be a universal urge. We spin our stories perhaps in part to stave off the haunting sense that life might be meaningless; but we tell our stories primarily because we're hardwired to do so. "When I was a little girl, I remember the time that my grandmother . . ." "Four years ago, the first time he walked into my office, I think I knew from the start that I loved him . . ."

And our unfinished stories do vary — your story is different from mine because of different life experiences. Even so, somehow or other we fit them into a Big Picture, we develop a sense of how our own stories fit into a larger one — historical, geographical, political, cosmic. We shape a coherent story out of the world we live in and the meaning of it all — even if it's not clearly thought out and expressed, even if, when pressed, we imagine the end of our world whimpering out into a black nothing. All of us have in our imaginative recesses at least a vague Big Picture of reality and its shape. And our individual Big Picture stories mesh well enough so that we can communicate and understand each other's imagined world, which we share on some basic communal level.

Of course, our own particular life stories are often haphazard, and certainly they are unfinished. We don't know how our particular tales will end. So maybe we find the stories we read and see enacted on screen or stage so very satisfying because they have not only a beginning but a middle and an end. They possess a form that completes the action, a wholeness and an integrity that our own lives do not yet have.

Probably most of us can remember being read to as a child. If you pause and think for a moment, you might recall the sense of safety, of security that many of these stories gave you because of their happy ending, with Cinderella getting the glass slipper — an ending where everything comes out right. In addition, I think that a second reason that novels are so popular in our modern culture is that a really good story has a *spiritual* impact on the reader, conveying a sense of personal growth as the fictional characters develop and change across the time frame of the plot. Many stories, whether for children or for adults, can subtly convey the advantages of moral behavior undergirded by spiritual meaning. Classic tales by Dickens and Dostoyevsky and Tolstoy, and, more recently, the work of Kent Haruf (e.g., *Plainsong*) and Anne Tyler (e.g., *A Patchwork Planet*) show a path to being whole and healed,

75

or at least a way to face the ordeals of life (as Buechner puts it our opening quote, "how to bear the weight of our own sadness").

In a sense, reading (as opposed to seeing a film or a play) is an intensely intimate act, with the reader engaging in an inner dialogue with the writer as well as with the characters in the story as it unfolds. Nancy Malone explains, "The act of reading is like the act of eating . . . a devouring of the words on the page, a taking into myself, the fulfillment of some elemental need."[2] This act rests on our imaginative capacity to engage the unseen other, to picture and feel the characters and to transcend what we are at this moment, to become potentially more in response to the story before us.

Malone quotes Kafka's ideas about reading in a letter he wrote to a friend:

> Altogether, I think we ought to read only books that bite and sting us. If the book we are reading doesn't shake us awake like a blow on the skull, why bother reading it in the first place? . . . What we need are books that hit us like a most painful misfortune, like the death of someone we loved more than we love ourselves. . . . A book must be the axe of the frozen sea within us. That is what I believe.[3]

A bit extreme, perhaps, but Kafka makes the point. A good book, or a good play or film, should make us think.

And what is highlighted in a good story is the concrete, the particular thing that is brought before us, the concrete person or interpersonal dilemma or inner conflict made vivid. The writer, the artist, in contrast with the scientist, philosopher, and theologian, focuses intensely on this particular and not the general thing or concept, focuses on King Lear and the meaning of his madness and the possibility of forgiveness and reconciliation with his daughter, not on the abstract nature of repentance and redemption per se. He or she throws light, creates and illumines a particular slant on human life, as if saying, to borrow St. Teresa's imperative, "I require you to look." And sometimes, in the looking, we are profoundly changed.

In fact, as Malone and others point out, engaging with a story is a

2. Nancy M. Malone, *Walking a Literary Labyrinth* (New York: Riverhead Books, 2003), p. 31.

3. Malone, *Walking a Literary Labyrinth,* pp. 117-18.

conversation, an exchange the reader has with the author ("Can I believe you? Do I trust what you are trying to persuade me to see?"), with the characters ("Oh, King Lear, don't be so foolish as to give all your kingdom away to such wretched creatures as your daughters appear to be!"), and with himself ("I've done just that kind of thing — and was so sorry"). Thus, the creativity of the writer or storyteller is not a one-way street. The reader co-creates in dialogue, self-transcending and being transformed in the process, imaginatively trying on identities as he responds in a relatively cost-free but potentially transforming way. That is, we can see in our imagination the end of a journey as the outcome of choices made, before we ourselves risk the voyage by the move we actually make.

In *The Revelatory Text,* Sandra Schneiders distinguishes between the world behind the text (the historical setting in which it was written, the author's intent in writing, the intended audience in that historical period, etc.), the world of the text (the genre — e.g., poetry, mystery prose, the classic Western film — and the shape of the plot, the character development, etc.), and the world before the text. This latter world before the text is the imagined world projected in the reader's mind, a new world created out of the experience of engagement with a great work of art.[4]

Sometimes this latter world is projected only temporarily, so that when the reader closes the book or walks out of the movie theater, the feeling flowing from the imagined world in which she immersed herself dissipates over time. But sometimes that world created by the imagination in response to the work is so absorbing and pivotal that the self becomes transformed in the process. Schneiders describes that experience in a particularly affecting way:

> A literary work clears a space, creates a world, into which the reader is invited. One difference between a good work and a poor one is that poor work never quite achieves a total world. One is aware that one is watching a play, or reading a novel. One does not become "lost" in the work. One's everyday world is not suspended and temporarily replaced by the new space, the new relationships, the new reality of the work. By contrast, after reading a great novel or seeing a fine play, one has the impression of having been in a different world for the duration of the artistic experience. The reader or spectator has experi-

4. Sandra M. Schneiders, *The Revelatory Text* (Collegeville, Minn.: Liturgical Press, 1999).

enced a whole range of emotion that is not related to or a response to everyday life. She or he has thought, not about the events and concerns of mundane existence, but about the issues of the novel or the play. One has established relationships with the characters and identified with or rejected the values proposed by the work. One cares deeply about what happens, how the plot works out and is finally resolved. One can come out of a play depressed and in tears or elated and renewed in hope. *One has lived a different life, in a different world, and returns to the reality of everyday life changed in some way.*[5]

The engaged reader or viewer then feels compelled to struggle with the existential significance of the work. He or she grapples with the questions that linger after reading *Dead Man Walking* or after seeing *King Lear,* questions about the sacredness of life, about justice, about forgiveness and redemption, about death. Engaged reading or viewing becomes a grappling with things that matter on many different levels — emotional, political, psychological, social, theological.

In the end we are talking about spiritual transformation, mediated by the imagination. Ultimately we are talking about the breaking in of Transcendence through our imaginative response to narrative art. As Catherine Wallace puts it, "Art and the reception of art are both works of grace and not mere human achievements."[6] The imagination plays a central role in our encounter with stories in all their forms, feeding our understanding and nourishing our appropriation of their meaning in the process of spiritual growth. The imagination is the gateway where human and divine truth — glimpsed through a good story's symbols and metaphors — intersect, transforming us in the process.

Nancy Malone speaks of "book providence" in this context. Certain books seem to come into our lives at particular times for perhaps a God-given, spiritually transformative purpose. As Schneiders and Wallace and others see it, once our imagination has been so touched, once our vision has been profoundly transformed, there is no going back.

5. Schneiders, *The Revelatory Text,* p. 167, emphasis added. For those interested in studying further the significance of narrative as theological method, an excellent resource is an earlier work edited by Stanley Hauerwas and L. Gregory Jones entitled *Why Narrative? Readings in Narrative Theology* (Grand Rapids: William B. Eerdmans, 1989).

6. Catherine Wallace, "Faith and Fiction: Literature as Revelation," *Anglican Theological Review* 78, no. 3 (1996): 401.

The transforming power of an imaginative response to a work of art — here, in the form of literature, film, or play — is of course of a piece with Coleridge's theory of the imagination as an opening onto Transcendence. As we saw in earlier chapters, Coleridge understood the creative writer's imagination as a power to perceive signs or symbols of transcendent truth inherent in the world around us and to then create and express through symbolic language new insights grasped by intuition. Then the artistic work thus created operates on the imaginative power of its engaged readers or viewers, who in turn create meaning within themselves in the process. As Wallace puts it, "An imaginative writer at the peak of his or her power elicits an imaginative response, despite particular . . . choices about genre. . . . Both reading well and writing well arise from the imagination."[7] Coleridge believed that it is through various art forms that we encounter God; this is the way the human imagination works.

In this discussion, I think it's important to remind ourselves that all of great literature — from the Bible to Shakespeare and beyond — and, more generally, all of the imagination's creative products can be conceived of as potentially revelatory, as conduits of God's revelation of God's Self and Truth.

Meeting God in the Story Told:
Glimmers of Transcendence in Novels, Films, and Theater

The term *postmodern* in its literary sense arose out of the field of literary criticism and the study of language itself. I do not intend here to undertake an in-depth discussion of literary theory, nor will I trace the development of such theory in all its historical turnings. Since I am not a literary critic, I am not prepared to do either. But in order for us to approach contemporary novels, films, and plays as they are created and then read or viewed, it is important for us to get some flavor of literary postmodernism in its present form.

Texts have come to be seen as endlessly open in meaning not only because of the questions addressed to them but because of the very nature of language itself. For the literary postmodernists, words simply signify other words, which in turn point to still other words, in infinite

---

7. Wallace, "Faith and Fiction," p. 390.

regression. But many have also come to see the potential presence of mystery through such absence of closure. Because what is *not* said, what the signifying words *imply* as "next," the not-said beyond the text has come to be seen as a haunting "presence" by its absence.

Thus, in terms of literary expression, irony has become a favored mode in much contemporary literature. Irony, after all, is an implying of what is *not* said ("Beautiful weather, isn't it?" when the day dawns rainy, nasty, and foul). And irony emerges as a very compatible manner of speaking in our fragmented, pluralistic culture. Irony in fact is a powerful form of expression because it says the opposite of what one means, relating in an oblique way to what lies outside the words of the text, floating "like something seen out of the corner of one's eye,"[8] like William James's reference to something that "twinkles," the Presence behind and beyond what is said.

Therefore, ironic stories — for example, the prose poems of T. S. Eliot and the short stories of Flannery O'Connor — can become vehicles of transformation nonetheless. Our imaginations can engage with paradoxically expressed truth beneath the symbols and metaphors given. We can then co-create meaning out of what is *not* said, grasping an underlying truth at the heart of the work.

Meeting God in Short Stories and Novels

In the 1950s Nathan Scott argued that the novel at mid-twentieth century carried the creative burden of meaning-making for most Americans, because the American theater was "moribund," and poetry was too esoteric for common consumption.[9] Whether this observation still holds is debatable, although a stroll through Barnes and Noble or Borders reveals a still-lively interest in prose fiction. But it may well be that films have superseded the popularity of novels in our quest for entertainment and discovery of life's significance within the story form. (I will have to defer to theater critics on the status, "moribund" or otherwise, of the current plays being produced on or off Broadway.)

8. Stephen Prickett, *Narrative, Religion, and Science* (New York: Cambridge University Press, 2002), p. 216.

9. Nathan Scott, *The Broken Center* (New Haven: Yale University Press, 1966).

Concerned primarily with fictional characters as individuals, and delving into characters' subjective worlds in a realistic way, the novel form that took hold in the late nineteenth century was born in an age of crumbling religious certainty, and was thus built on the ruins of religious belief. Writing in the year 2000, David McLaurin sees the contemporary cultural setting for the novel as devoid of moral or religious signposts or direction.[10]

Although this seems to be the case for the most part, the novels we will consider here do grapple with life's great religious themes: death and dying, ecstasy and conversion, evil and goodness, forgiveness and redemption. Perhaps for inhabitants of the twenty-first century, the most powerful way of disclosing transcendent meaning may be the most indirect — namely, through good fiction.

I for one am an insatiable reader of novels, consuming at least one a week. Usually it takes a chapter or so before I become lost in the story, really engaged with the characters as people I'm getting to know, beginning to care about them and what happens to them as individuals. So it was hard for me to select the few we could focus on here. I considered and then passed over some of the classic nineteenth-century realistic works by Dostoyevsky (e.g., *The Idiot*) and Tolstoy (e.g., *The Death of Ivan Ilych*). The latter is a particularly gripping account of one man's life "most ordinary, and therefore most terrible." This novella is still hailed by many critics as the classic portrayal of coming to grips with death and glimpsing through suffering what it means to be human.

There are other, more contemporary candidates that I considered for inclusion here, books that stimulated my imagination to see the world in a deeper, truer light, books within whose world I lost myself — reminding me of some truth about being human, shining some transcendent light onto my everyday world beyond the story, being revelatory in the truest sense of the word. Choices within this enchanted category included Kent Haruf's *Plainsong* — a wonderful story of two old bachelor farmers who make room in their enclosed life for an unwed teenage mother, revealing the meaning of human, familial love as well as transcendent, sacrificial love at its deepest core. Similarly, Oscar

---

10. David McLaurin, "The Dark Night of the Novel in an Age of Weak Faith," in *The Novel, Spirituality, and Modern Culture,* ed. Paul Fiddes (Llandybie, Great Britain: Dinefwr Press, 2000).

Hijuelos's *Mr. Ives' Christmas* was a strong candidate. It's the story of a deeply religious man whose life becomes haunted by the murder of his son. The story depicts the man's struggle of faith against the depression and despair oppressing his decades of mourning, his anguish when finally he is called upon to meet the murderer after his release from prison, and his final grace-sustained ability to do so as a result of his faith practice over a lifetime. Hijuelos's beautiful work imaginatively displays the triumph of the human spirit sustained by Transcendence in the end. Also in the running were Annie Proulx's *The Shipping News* and David Guterson's *Snow Falling on Cedars*. If you're a reader of fiction, I'm sure you can supply your own favorite list.

Finally, I needed to make a choice. Here I've chosen to focus on two stories: one a short parable and the other a novel that was itself a blessing to read.

Flannery O'Connor's "Revelation"

Many have seen O'Connor's writings as shocking and ugly. She aimed at picturing the world, for all its evil and sordidness, as not absolutely depraved but as undergirded by God's grace, shot through with spiritual meaning. O'Connor used extreme images to shout this truth because she felt that her readers were deaf to transcendent meaning otherwise, "embarrassed by Mystery."[11] Many of her stories, including this one, are ironic parables through which the reader's imagination can grasp a paradoxical reality quite the opposite from the world that the characters assume to be true. And grace breaks in by surprising means, often through characters who are themselves deeply flawed and grotesque examples of near — but not absolute — depravity. Thus, a divine truth is glimpsed: God uses even the banal, the imperfect, and on occasion the truly evil ones to achieve God's ends.

The setting for this particular story is a waiting room in a doctor's office.[12] The protagonist, a Mrs. Turpin, is a classic O'Connor character, a smug, judgmental woman who sizes up everyone else in the world

---

11. Helpful for my discussion here was T. R. Wright's treatment of O'Connor's work in his *Theology and Literature* (Oxford: Blackwell Publishing, 1988).

12. Flannery O'Connor, "Revelation," in *Flannery O'Connor: The Complete Stories* (New York: Noonday Press, 1972), pp. 488-509.

and is thankful that she is better than most. White, middle-class, entrenched in and thus reflective of a world of racial bigotry, she is sanctimonious and utterly blind to her own narrow prejudice — in this case, aimed at "white trash" (examples of which sit with her in the waiting room) and the "niggers" she and her husband hire to take care of their small cotton crop.

In the course of a conversation between Mrs. Turpin and another woman in the waiting room, the plot builds toward a climax as the woman's college-age daughter, who is sitting with her, malevolently stares at Mrs. Turpin. Her loathing for Mrs. Turpin and all she stands for becomes palpable, and finally, when she can no longer stand Mrs. Turpin's hypocrisy, the girl hurls a book at Mrs. Turpin's head (a textbook on "human development"!), knocking her to the floor of the waiting room.

As Mrs. Turpin lies there, stunned, she finally asks the girl why she's been singled out for such violence. "'What you got to say to me?' she asked hoarsely and held her breath, waiting, as for a revelation." The answer coming from the girl's mouth shakes Mrs. Turpin to the core: "Go back to hell where you came from, you old wart hog."[13]

And for the rest of this story, Mrs. Turpin is haunted by those words, struggling to understand how that girl could have said such a thing to her, she who has always been nothing but the picture of kindness and decency in the self-satisfied world she has inhabited. She struggles with herself and she struggles with God — who, after all, has made her what she is.

By the last scene, where Mrs. Turpin is seen slopping her own pigs on her farm, she has worked herself into a fury. She turns on God himself with the question "Who do you think you are?" And in the following mysterious moments, with that question seemingly turned back upon herself, she gazes "as if through the very heart of mystery," and her own sense of righteous integrity begins to crumble. While staring at the pigs in the pen before her, some truth about herself and about life and about sheer reality begins to dawn on her, "as if she was absorbing some abysmal life-giving knowledge." At that moment, she lifts her eyes and sees the following vision:

---

13. O'Connor, "Revelation," p. 500.

A visionary light settled in her eyes. She saw the streak as a vast swinging bridge extending upward from the earth through a field of living fire. Upon it a vast horde of souls were rumbling toward heaven. There were whole companies of white-trash, clean for the first time in their lives, and bands of black niggers in white robes, and battalions of freaks and lunatics shouting and clapping and leaping like frogs. And bringing up the end of the procession was a tribe of people whom she recognized at once as those who, like herself and Claud, had always had a little of everything and the God-given wit to use it right. She leaned forward to observe them closer. They were marching behind the others with great dignity, accountable as they had always been for good order and common sense and respectable behavior. They alone were on key. Yet she could see by their shocked and altered faces that even their virtues were being burned away.[14]

O'Connor does not tell us whether this revelatory vision of profound reversal — the first will be last and the last will be first — makes any real difference in Mrs. Turpin's life. Even at this moment of Transcendence, she still views others in some kind of fixed hierarchy.

But readers, now imaginatively engaged with this character, are left with the sense of possibility, for Mrs. Turpin and perhaps for themselves. Maybe things aren't just what they seem; maybe just beneath the surface of life's order is another, profound God-given order which, if only we could see it and remember it, would alter our perception of and behavior toward others. The last line of the story reads, ". . . what she heard were the voices of the souls climbing upward into the starry field and shouting hallelujah."[15] Perhaps in the end we will all rejoice — even the Mrs. Turpins of the world.

Mark Salzman's Lying Awake

The setting for this novel is a Carmelite monastery near present-day Los Angeles.[16] It is the story of Sister John of the Cross, who, after more than two decades of religious life, becomes something of a celebrity. After years of spiritual dryness and plodding along within the monastery

14. O'Connor, "Revelation," pp. 507-8.
15. O'Connor, "Revelation," p. 508.
16. Mark Salzman, *Lying Awake* (New York: Alfred A. Knopf, 2000).

confines, she becomes a visionary, given to mystical experiences of God. When she writes about her mystical experience, her published poetry and essays bring personal recognition and monetary reward to her monastery.

Unfortunately, it turns out that Sister John's increasing "mystical experiences," accompanied by increasingly severe headaches, are manifestations of a form of temporal lobe epilepsy. She is faced with the choice of undergoing surgery and the likely loss of her visionary power, or risking increasingly severe neurological consequences that would endanger her life. This is the dilemma at the heart of Salzman's novel.

Readers, through the power of their imaginations, glimpse a world of loving and humble service beneath the everyday responsibilities of communal life. Along with Sister John, they begin to discover through the course of her illness and its treatment the true meaning of religious faith and life in a community of others that one is called to serve. Sister John's struggle is the struggle of a faith stripped bare of emotional consolation, stripped of pride in spiritual attainment, stripped of false highs amid the everydayness of life. At one point, when she is face-to-face with her dilemma, her spiritual advisor says to her, "You may feel separated from grace right now, but in reality you are probably closer to it now than you ever were before. . . . We're all better off having doubts about the state of our souls than presuming ourselves to be holy."[17]

Out of Sister John's struggle there emerges a picture of a life lived in true faith as one ultimately lived in mystery and darkness, a "doing kind of knowing" that lives out faith in living for others, hanging in there and living by faith despite doubts and everyday dryness of soul. Perhaps, as one of the sisters says to Sister John, "If we make an act of faith then [when it's all dry darkness], it counts more than on the days when we feel sure."[18] Perhaps the title, *Lying Awake,* symbolizes such living in darkness.

Toward the end of this story, while Sister John is still in the infirmary recovering from her surgery, still mourning the loss of her mystical muse, a very old nun, doubled over with osteoporosis, is serving the other sick sisters. She pauses next to Sister John's bed and says, "God

17. Salzman, *Lying Awake,* p. 125.
18. Salzman, *Lying Awake,* p. 172.

showed you what heaven could be like, and you shared it with others. Now you can do something even better."

"You think so?" Sister John asks.

Mother Mary Joseph nods. "Walk in faith even though heaven seems out of reach. Think how good it would be if you could write about that." And then she says, "Everything we learn about God leads to deeper mystery. Hard to accept sometimes, but we have to keep going."[19]

Through the power of the imagination weaving together the characters' images with your own memory's store of background experience and tradition's teachings, perhaps you as reader can "try on" for yourself a life walking in faith despite doubt, finding God in loving service — even when heaven seems far out of reach. Your imagination takes the story as a metaphor for a life in community with others whom you put up with as they put up with you, holding on for God's sake, loving and forgiving as you go along. Through your imagination, at least you can glimpse what such a faith-filled life — captured in the symbolic figure of Sister John — would look like. And such an imaginative encounter with truth beneath metaphor could change you for good.

Salzman's novel is one of those stories that I think has something important to say to those who hunger for faith and wind up with a handful of self-questioning doubts. There is mystery and there is meaning beneath the surface of the everyday, and novels such as this one imaginatively open onto that mystery and give hope on life's mostly mundane journey.

Meeting God in Film

Both film and theater are powerful visual displays of imaginative worlds. And for all the junk now showing on screens (especially the small ones in our living rooms) and perhaps onstage, some masterpieces have emerged in these forms along the way that do speak to some truth about human existence. As we will see when we take a look at several examples, such imaginative works of art glimmer and hint at something more — some deeper transcendent meaning — beyond the story produced.

19. Salzman, *Lying Awake*, p. 175.

And so we come first to film. Almost everyone goes to the movies! In fact, young people between the ages of sixteen and twenty-five regularly attend the local movie theater, with the very young and the older not so far behind. Making movies has become a very big business: blockbuster films like the Harry Potter series are box-office hits that bring in millions of dollars. But films are more than that; they are an American art form that has become one of the ways that we tell our stories. Like some novels, some movies can be revelatory of Transcendence.

While novels stimulate the imaginative production of images within our own consciousness, movies present us with powerful visual stimuli, images larger than life. We find ourselves seated in a darkened theater, analogous to the sacred space of a church, and are drawn into the images and sounds that surround us.

As with literary criticism, in film criticism there is an entire technical area of film analysis having to do with plot, atmosphere, tone, framing, and special effects, which I will not detail here.[20] Suffice it to say that when these elements come together, films have an immediate potency that probably exceeds the power of novels. Movies can produce strong reactions in viewers because they use both visual images and words, sights and sounds that stimulate the senses, augmenting their emotional and visceral impact with music, color, architecture, and movement.

Unlike books, movies are experienced in a specific time frame. You can't lay a movie down and pick it up again at your convenience (unless you rent a DVD and watch it on your TV or computer screen at home — a completely different experience from communal viewing in a darkened theater within a two-hour time frame). And within that specified, delimited period of time, viewers are taken on an experiential journey.

Books usually probe the inner subjective world of the characters in a direct way; films probe their characters' inner world indirectly through action (or through the occasional use of voice overlay). Movies are also accessible in a way that novels sometimes are not. You can't read a book that you don't understand. But you can watch a movie without fully understanding it and be both entertained and pro-

---

20. If you're interested in film analysis, a good place to begin is with Robert Johnston's *Reel Spirituality* (Grand Rapids: Baker Academic, 2004).

voked to ask questions about its meaning. As one critic notes, "Movies are felt by the audience long before they are understood . . . if indeed they are ever fully understood."[21]

Powerful films can indeed reach into our souls and provoke our imaginations to wonder about the glimmers of truth we glimpse there. There are many such good movies from which to select for our discussion. Among them I would list Steven Spielberg's *Schindler's List* and *Saving Private Ryan,* Robert Duvall's *The Apostle,* Miloš Forman's *One Flew Over the Cuckoo's Nest,* George Clooney's *Good Night and Good Luck,* and Gabriel Axel's art film *Babette's Feast.* But for my purposes here, I've chosen Martin Scorsese's *The Last Temptation of Christ.*[22]

Scorsese's 1988 film was based on Nikos Kazantzakis's novel by the same name. The novel, published in 1955, had been placed on the index of forbidden books by the Catholic Church. The film was very controversial. I remember seeing it in Pittsburgh, standing in a line of theatergoers while protestors picketed the movie theater within twenty feet of the box office.

Although "Christ films" have appeared at least since the early twentieth century, and have included classics such as George Stevens's *The Greatest Story Ever Told* (1965) and Franco Zeffirelli's *Jesus of Nazareth* (1977), *The Last Temptation* depicts Jesus as the most human of figures.

As William Telford points out, portraying Jesus Christ in a movie presents a number of difficulties for a film director. The choice of actor, for one thing, can be problematic — as he says, you can't imagine Danny DeVito in the role! In addition, leading men usually capture the audience's attention through acts of sex or violence, and mostly the Jesus of the Gospels is neither sexual nor violent. And it's hard to portray someone as both human and divine. How do you portray divinity on the screen?[23]

21. J. R. May, quoted by David John Graham, "The Uses of Film in Theology," in *Explorations in Theology and Film,* ed. Clive Marsh and Gaye Ortiz (Malden, Mass.: Blackwell Publishing, 2004), p. 38.

22. In 2004 Mel Gibson produced *The Passion of the Christ.* This movie was as controversial as *The Last Temptation.* Many reviewers were quite critical of what they saw as its gratuitous violence, and some found it blatantly anti-Semitic. For this reason, I am not discussing it here.

23. William R. Telford, "Jesus Christ, Movie Star: The Depiction of Jesus in the Cinema," in Marsh and Ortiz, *Explorations in Theology and Film,* pp. 115-41.

In Scorsese's film, divinity was not obvious. What was finally depicted was a very human Jesus — at times doubting and indecisive, a man wracked by anxiety and guilt for his own failings as well as for those of others, a man who struggled with his mission. This portrayal was controversial, to say the least.

One could argue that these human facets are not entirely absent from the Gospel narratives. Mark's Jesus in particular is shown to be emotional and occasionally distressed, angry and impatient, harsh with his family and others, and in fact is thought to be mad by some. Telford says, "What makes him the Christ — for Scorsese, for Kazantzakis, and arguably for the Gospels also — is his victory in this struggle of spirit over flesh, mind over matter, good over evil. In that respect, he is a salvific figure, 'a prototype of the free man,' a savior for a new age."[24]

Many people boycotted this movie, and a number of critics, particularly religious critics, excoriated the production. Perhaps chief among their complaints was that Jesus was presented as sexualized, with physical longings for Mary Magdalene. The "last temptation," of course, was the image of domesticity, of normal family life with a wife and children, which Jesus finally rejected from the cross for the sake of fulfilling his mission as he saw it.

I remember being deeply affected by this film — its images, its symbolism, its metaphoric portrayal of the human struggle to hear God's word in the face of bewilderingly bad odds. While many took issue with Mel Gibson's depiction of the crucifixion scene in *The Passion of the Christ,* I found the crucifixion scene in *The Last Temptation* in no way offensive. It was a powerful portrayal of the death of Jesus Christ — an event in history that became, whether one is religious or not, of pivotal significance for the whole civilized world then and since.

But the point here is that this movie also fed the imaginations of those who saw it, not only provoking questions about Christ's mission, life, and death, questions regarding his purpose and end, but also provoking questions about the relationship between sexuality and holiness, about human motivation in the face of evil, about self-sacrifice.

Scorsese's intention was to make the person of Jesus accessible to people's imaginations, to enable viewers to engage with the Jesus

24. Telford, "Jesus Christ, Movie Star," p. 137.

Christ of history, to make the Gospel story come alive for twentieth-century moviegoers. Telford comments, "In an age which has demystified its saints, removed its icons from their pedestals, and demoted its heroes, it is fitting that the more realistic and introspective Christ of the 1990's, as brought to us by Scorsese, should share our human capacity for doubt as well as faith, for skepticism as well as hope, and that his struggle, if it is to be ours, should be seen as both real and genuine."[25]

Filmmakers, as well as novelists and other artists, create out of their own culture and speak to their own times. Like Flannery O'Connor's stories, Scorsese's film unsettled and startled people with its images, provoking imaginative responses in many who hadn't thought about God for a long time.

Meeting God in the Theater

Just as there are many movies being produced and many viewers flocking to see them, so there are many plays being produced — on and off Broadway, at local venues — some stupid or banal, some valuable. Among those that are valuable, some raise important questions, and a few show a depth of meaning that is truly profound.

Many stage and film productions are revelatory. But I think the question for us becomes — revelatory of what? What kinds of questions are raised in the viewer's mind? What is the reality imaginatively created in the mind's eye, when the viewer pieces and blends together a world of meaning in response? Is that glimpsed reality finally utterly absurd, a world of "waiting for Godot" who will never come, reinforcing a sense of humanity desperate to believe but incapable of any religious faith?

I do not believe that bleakness characterizes the current scene. But I do believe that we live in a time of skepticism, what T. R. Wright calls a time of "probing those hard facts of life with which faith has to reckon," a time that may be most conducive to the tragic in story form. As Wright points out, tragic art — in this case, plays — usually does not deny the very possibility of religious faith or ultimate meaning, but

---

25. Telford, "Jesus Christ, Movie Star," p. 138.

struggles with questions of human limits, of guilt and sin, of finitude and death, of self-destruction and inner integrity.[26]

The focus for tragedy is therefore humanity, but human beings caught in a world of mysterious and inexorable power which they cannot prevail against and which they cannot fully understand. As Nathan Scott puts it,

> What is bitter and ironic is that precisely in thus choosing himself and assuming the burden of his own destiny, the tragic man becomes a guilty man. For his commitment to the truth as he sees it is, inevitably, a commitment to a truth that is something less than the Whole Truth: he is finite, his perspectives are limited, his standpoint can never in the nature of the case afford a sufficiently spacious view of his total situation . . . — that is to say, in the quest for meaning, man is at a fundamental disadvantage simply by reason of being human.[27]

I think of Job, railing against God's injustice, demanding an accountability from God for the evil that has befallen him and his family. At the heart of such protest, at the dynamic source of tragic action, is human pride. Man asserts himself out of pride, and ultimately he loses — but he learns something of crucial importance in the process.

Some argue that there can be no true tragedy written or produced today because modern people have lost their moral base and thus are incapable of feeling personal guilt following their prideful protest, are capable only of experiencing anxiety. Some even argue that the American theater is dead because the matters taken up in modern plays provide banal entertainment at best. Despite these arguments, at least one clear example of a modern tragedy comes to my mind: Arthur Miller's *The Crucible* (and perhaps also his *Death of a Salesman*). Maybe the reader can think of other examples. But for our purposes here, I want to focus on *The Crucible* and the world it creates.

When *The Crucible* was first produced on Broadway in the early 1950s, it was the height of the McCarthy era in American politics and public life, with McCarthy becoming famous for his witch hunts for communist sympathizers. Miller sought a parallel situation in American life for his play's setting, and chose the witch trials in seventeenth-

26. Wright, *Theology and Literature,* p. 178.
27. Scott, *The Broken Center,* p. 127.

century Salem, Massachusetts.[28] He saw in both McCarthyism and Puritan fanaticism stories of intolerance that whip up mass hysteria for their own evil purposes.

Postwar American theater, with plays by major writers such as Miller and Tennessee Williams, along with earlier works by Eugene O'Neill, was essentially dark and gloomy, focusing on psychological forces and pathological motives. But Miller's work was also basically a social commentary on contemporary culture, with moralistic intent. I saw *The Crucible* presented on stage about four years ago, and it was a gripping experience.

The basic issue in this play involves the struggle for the human right to self-determination — the right to defend oneself against destruction brought on by forced conformity rationalized as defending right-mindedness and decency. You could argue that such social forces are still at work today.

In Miller's preface to the script, he observes that the dilemma depicted in this play is one that lies at the base of all social organization. Because in order for communities to cohere and maintain themselves, by definition they must exclude and prohibit the unacceptable deviant. When individual freedom is exercised, witch hunts ensue. Miller says, "When one rises above the individual villainy displayed [in this play's characters], one can only pity them all, just as we shall be pitied some day. It is still impossible for man to organize his social life without repressions, and the balance has yet to be struck between order and freedom."[29]

Because this is such a masterfully created play, the audience can become caught up in its world, discovering some deep truth about being human in the process. The theater where I saw it produced was designed to allow the audience to sit facing three sides of the action. I happened to be sitting in the front-row center of the "U" shape, so I could almost physically reach out and touch the world that was opening before me, could almost smell the fear of the characters as they faced their own mortality — many of them with courage and grace. In the world displayed before me, I became one of them.

The story is a powerful one. A handful of impressionable teenage girls falls prey to mass hysteria, claiming to have come under the devil's

---

28. Arthur Miller, *The Crucible* (New York: Bantam Books, 1968).
29. Miller, *The Crucible*, p. 5.

spell. One by one others get denounced, and the guilty circle widens, until not only the girls but some of the town's most upstanding citizens are pulled into a net of accusations.

The protagonist is a nonconformist named John Proctor. And Proctor is the classic tragic character. Like King Lear, he comes to own his own fallibility, admitting his sinful past of lust and unfaithfulness to his wife (who has also been falsely accused of witchcraft along the way and awaits her own hanging once their unborn child is delivered). Having also been denounced as being in league with the devil, Proctor is likewise imprisoned. Struggling with his human desire to live and save himself by lying (to confess to witchery as a repentant sinner, implicating and thus condemning others in the process), Proctor finally tells the magistrate that "I will have my life." But he sees his embrace of the lie as evil, and he cries out to heaven, "God in Heaven, what is John Proctor? What is John Proctor?"[30] At that moment he sees that he is no saint, that he cannot be a saint, that even if he remains silent and does not tell the lie, it will make no difference — he still cannot be a saint. Whether he tells it or not, it is all the same. He is no saint. He embraces evil at that moment in his desperation to live.

However, Proctor does refuse to sign and have posted on the church door his written "confession." In the most affecting lines of this play, when pressed as to why he will not let his name be displayed, he cries out, "Because it is my name! Because I cannot have another in my life! Because I lie and sign myself to lies! Because I am not worth the dust on the feet of them that hang! How may I live without my name? I have given you my soul; leave me my name!"[31]

Realizing that he will now hang, Proctor glimpses some truth about himself, perhaps by grace-filled intuition sensing the meaning beneath his refusal to sign his name — that name being a symbol of his core integrity. He says to the presiding cleric, "You have made your magic now, for now I do think I see some shred of goodness in John Proctor. Not enough to weave a banner with, but white enough to keep it from such dogs."[32]

And so, in classic tragic style, Proctor goes to his death having

30. Miller, *The Crucible,* p. 132.
31. Miller, *The Crucible,* p. 138.
32. Miller, *The Crucible,* p. 138.

learned an important truth about himself. In response to St. Teresa's "I require you to look," he confronts and resists the evil forces within which he is caught, and he discovers some sense of human truth — some personal salvation beyond the struggle.

It is true that this play is utterly humanistic, despite its world of religious symbols and language of sin and guilt, its allusions to God's knowing our inner thoughts and forgiveness. Miller intends an imaginative protest against the use of human institutions for evil human purposes. Unlike *King Lear,* the forces here are not the gods or finally God himself. And the railings are not against death and human finitude and innocent suffering brought about by arbitrary divine will. They are railings against institutional power, which has the potential and the proclivity to choke life out of those who will not go along with the program.

But this play creates an imaginative world that engaged viewers confront — a world that can unsettle our comfort with institutional arrangements that have the self-serving power to crush nonconforming protest in the name of security or religious righteousness. And so questions are provoked as we are also required to look. For example, is our freedom as citizens now being compromised too much in the name of civil security?

But more than that, if all forms of art can be means of grace, this play carries with it perhaps a yearning for goodness. Would I, like John Proctor, see some vision beyond my own mortal life, glimpse some truth worth dying for? In this play and others by Miller and other contemporary playwrights — in their confrontation of the "disorders of modern life," as Scott phrases it — "there is implicit perhaps a kind of intuition of the Sacred, the kind of sentiment of Being, that the literature of our period offers us."[33]

As I have stressed from the beginning, what you ultimately make of such a play in terms of transcendent significance — just as what you make of ritual gesture or poetic symbol — depends on an imagination rooted in a tradition of meaning that shapes those images and thus your worldview. The specific point here is that there are still plays written and produced that open up a conduit for grace, providing a vehicle for transcendent revelation.

33. Scott, *The Broken Center,* p. 185.

Meeting God in the Story of Scripture

There are many ways to read the Bible, which of course is not really one book but many books, written by different authors for different purposes and peoples over a very complex social and political history. The Christian Bible, finally collected into the books as we now know them in the fifth century, appropriated Hebrew texts, written hundreds of years before John wrote his book of Revelation, collected and interpreted for Christian purposes.[34]

I'm not going to review this complex history; instead, I'm going to consider the Bible as a grand story, a story of humans and our relation to a transcendent Creator who bothers himself with us and our history — what Catherine Fox calls "the only story broad enough and deep enough to bear the weight of human tragedy and disaster as well as human love and joy — to catch them up and make some sense of them."[35]

The Bible has been referred to as "historicized prose fiction," because it is both history and art.[36] It is based on history — to a certain extent at least. Historically the Jews were slaves in Egypt for a time, before migrating to the land of Israel; there probably was a King Saul and a King David; the grand Jerusalem temple was destroyed at some point around 70 A.D.; and the Jewish diaspora can be traced to Babylonian and Assyrian exile. For believing Christians, the heart of their faith is the historical concreteness of a person, a Galilean named Jesus, who came to be seen as the Christ or God's Anointed One. That is, Jesus was born at the time of Caesar Augustus, and was crucified under Pontius Pilate, and in the meantime, he was an itinerant preacher and healer. There was also a historical someone named Paul who had been a Jewish Pharisee and who wrote letters to the fledgling Christian communities.

But the stories in the New Testament as well as in the Old are also fictionalized works of art, written imaginatively by authors for certain

34. See, for example, Richard Hays, *The Conversion of the Imagination: Paul as Interpreter of Israel's Scripture* (Grand Rapids: William B. Eerdmans, 2005); Walter Brueggemann, *An Introduction to the Old Testament: The Canon and Christian Imagination* (Louisville: Westminster John Knox Press, 2003); and Walter Brueggemann, *The Prophetic Imagination* (Minneapolis: Augsburg Fortress Press, 2001).

35. Catherine Fox, "Telling the Old, Old Story: God and the Novelist as Creators," in Fiddes, *The Novel, Spirituality, and Modern Culture,* p. 101.

36. Robert Alter, *The Art of Biblical Narrative* (New York: Basic Books, 1981), p. 24.

purposes. These authors drew from historically based traditions that had been handed down to them, but they also created "history" by drawing on symbols, metaphors, myths, fables, and legends that were part of their culture at the time. They filled in the historical gaps, supplying dialogue and narrative interpretation out of their own rich imaginations to convey some revelatory truth as they saw it.

Reading these stories in the Bible as you would read any other stories, you can look at character development, plot, story transitions, heroes and villains, scene shifts and plot climaxes, tension and background tone, narration versus dialogue.[37] Read the story of King David and his court (2 Samuel 2–1 Kings 2) as an example of gripping intrigue and plot development. In fact, all that I have said in this chapter about reading prose fiction holds in reading the Bible as a collection of stories (as well as poetry and other genres). And again, all good stories, including the ones we read in the Bible, feed our imaginations and can affect us deeply; they are potential conduits of grace-filled images that color the world before us and shape our lives.

But of course the Bible is not like just any other book or books that we have considered up until now in a number of ways. First, for religious believers, in any case, these biblical writers are seen as inspired by God to set down God's particular dealings with humankind in history — responding as best they could with limited perspectives to the mighty acts of God — imaginatively describing as best they could the "unfathomability of life in history under an inscrutable God."[38]

Thus, these inspired authors wrote fictionalized history for readers who also could respond in only finite ways to ultimate and infinite mystery. Given our understanding that revelation through the prism of our imagination is ultimately God's revelation of God's self to humans, you might agree with Robert Alter that the author of the Bible is ultimately God. Thus, the ultimate background of this story — the unseen Author — is omniscient, mysterious, and divine. But within the pages of the written and the read, given our finite minds as they contend with such mystery, there is ambiguity and paradox.

---

37. See Alter, *The Art of Biblical Narrative*. For a greater in-depth look at the Bible as literature, see David Jasper and Stephen Prickett, *The Bible and Literature* (Oxford: Blackwell Publishing, 1999).

38. Alter, *The Art of Biblical Narrative*, p. 24.

Second, the Bible is not just another story because it contains stories of our ancestors in the faith — at least those in the Judeo-Christian and Muslim traditions. In that sense, it is like a family album that is treasured because it depicts all those who have gone before and have left a heritage for us to live by — a sacred record of God's doing in time and history. But as is always the case with our own families, our biblical ancestors were a mixed lot. Take, for example, the Old Testament figure of Jacob — a scheming scoundrel who connived to steal his brother's birthright and who proved to be a sly fox from the start. Is Jacob a sinner through and through, or just human with feet of clay like the rest of us, finally blessed by God as he is renamed Israel (Gen. 32:22-31)? The Bible, which D. H. Lawrence called "a great, confused novel," is filled with such characters.

And finally, of course, unlike other works of fiction we have discussed in this chapter, the Bible is the church's book. True, all who read it do so through the eyes of their own cultural and personal history. But the interpretations of the biblical text should be understood in light of the writer's original intent and be set within the stretchable bounds of Judeo-Christian tradition ("stretchable" in the sense that tradition develops dynamically over time). Not anything and everything goes when it comes to confronting the world within the biblical text and imaginatively making something of it.

Therefore, this set of stories found within the Old and New Testaments is seen by people of faith as sacred, as particular and unique, as an especially intense shining of revelatory light on the meaning of being human through the characters portrayed, reflecting hidden meaning in a world created by and shot through with transcendent grace.

And what is the story told from Genesis to Revelation — this story that begins where time begins and ends with the end of it all? What is the imagined reality, the sweep of the picture found in Scripture? One way to view the story of the Bible is to see it as the story of God's dealing with the humans God created as free agents. Within this frame, the authors of the Bible attempt to show God's purpose through historical events, but a purpose deeply complicated by human disorder, freedom, and finiteness. In this sense, the biblical writers tell the human story through particular cases and characters, as Alter explains:

[What is it like to be a human] with a divided consciousness — intermittently loving your brother but hating him even more; resentful or

97

perhaps contemptuous of your father but also capable of the deepest filial regard; stumbling between disastrous ignorance and imperfect knowledge; fiercely asserting your own independence but caught in a tissue of events divinely contrived; outwardly a definite character and inwardly an unstable vortex of greed, ambition, jealousy, lust, piety, courage, compassion, and much more? Fiction fundamentally serves the biblical writers as an instrument of fine insight into these abiding perplexities of man's creaturely condition.[39]

And so, in the last analysis, as Alter and others have stressed, the Bible is a book about us. We imagine ourselves in the fictionalized characters that we meet there — the farmers and the fishermen, the thieves and the traitors, the Good Samaritan and the Prodigal Son, the servants and the scribes. In short, we see women and men of all sorts and conditions who manage, like us, to be both good and bad, sometimes wondrously or disastrously so. Finally, as David Jasper points out, the Bible's stories have the quality of "frictionality" — "irritating qualities which drive us to scratch and read again, aware that there are traces left which never yield"[40] to any final or fixed form.

But the Central Character, as well as Author, who hovers over and behind the text is of course God. As someone has said, "The Bible without God is as unimaginable as Moby Dick without the whale." This is finally God's book, the One who is not seen directly but who is glimpsed in the lives of the characters who encountered him, and in the imaginations of those inspired to set down these stories that shaped their lives and that ultimately shape our own.

Whether you read it or not, the Bible permeates our culture with images and meanings. Whether you are Bible-literate or not, you know what it means to call someone a "Judas" or to use the phrase "the mark of Cain" as a sign of guilt. Titles of novels such as *East of Eden* and *Gilead* make reference to biblical images, and you miss a lot if you don't catch the full meaning. And if you happen to know any of the more familiar stories in the Bible, then you know that the novels, the films, and the play that we've looked at here speak to some of them.

For example, that last vision in O'Connor's story "Revelation,"

39. Alter, *The Art of Biblical Narrative,* p. 176.
40. David Jasper, "Literary Readings of the Bible: Trends in Modern Criticism," in Jasper and Prickett, *The Bible and Literature,* p. 60.

where "whole companies of white-trash . . . and battalions of freaks and lunatics" led the procession up to heaven, might bring to mind the parable of the laborers, where those who showed up to work in the vineyard at the end of the day got paid as much as those who'd labored all day long in the hot sun. Perhaps it doesn't seem fair that the last should be equal to the first, but then the Landlord can dispense payment as he sees fit! Or Mrs. Turpin's perverted and inflated self-estimation might bring to mind the Pharisee standing in the temple, giving thanks to God that he is not like other men — like the poor tax collector standing in the back, beating his chest.

But of course, the metaphors and ironic paradoxes expressed in fictional literary works raise questions, in turn, that we can pose *to* Scripture. The resulting dialogue can be a fruitful one, extending our reach for truth in our lives. The teenage girl in O'Connor's story is pictured as truly nasty. Can such a one be an instrument of God's grace? Are there *any* last who will *not* make it to first? How about Hitler? How about Bin Laden? Is God's love truly universal? Is repentance required? Is anyone beyond help? Beyond redemption?

So the dialogue between art and Scripture is mutually fruitful, engaging our imaginations and prompting questions that become openings for grace-filled insight. Let's look at one more example to end our discussion on imaginatively meeting God in the stories of Scripture — a fitting end, as this passage from Revelation reflects the end of it all in the last book of the Bible.

The theologian N. T. Wright has pictured the Bible — at least for the Christian — as a story or a play with five acts: Creation; the Fall; Israel's story; Jesus' life, death, and resurrection; and finally, the play's end. And it is that end which we stare into with only a vague image, an ambiguous picture of both our personal ends and the end of it all:

> Then I saw a new heaven and a new earth; for the first heaven and the first earth had passed away, and the sea was no more. And I saw the holy city, the new Jerusalem, coming down out of heaven from God, prepared as a bride adorned for her husband. And I heard a loud voice from the throne saying, "See, the home of God is among mortals. He will dwell with them as their God; they will be his peoples, and God himself will be with them; he will wipe away every tear from their eyes. Death will be no more; mourning and crying

and pain will be no more, for the first things have passed away." And the one who was seated on the throne said, "See, I am making all things new." Also he said, "Write this, for these words are trustworthy and true." Then he said to me, "It is done! I am the Alpha and the Omega, the beginning and the end. To the thirsty I will give water as a gift from the spring of the water of life. Those who conquer will inherit these things, and I will be their God, and they will be my children." (Rev. 21:1-7, NRSV)

Thus at the very end of the Bible the seer of Patmos sees this image of a whole new creation. At the very beginning of the Bible, God created the heavens and the earth, and now this first creation has passed away, and all the elements of chaos have been abolished — even death, which will be no more. The Christ has come into his own as the Alpha and the Omega — the first and last letters of the Greek alphabet, the beginning and end of it all.

This vision of the end has filled literary imaginations throughout history. Consider Milton's *Paradise Lost* and Coleridge's "Kubla Kahn" (which we looked at in the last chapter); Tolstoy's Ivan Ilych and his vision at death ("In place of death there was light. . . . 'Death is finished,' he said to himself. 'It is no more.'"); and contemporary science-fiction films such as *ET* and *Close Encounters of the Third Kind.* But this scene in Revelation, like any good imaginative artwork, raises more questions than it answers.

At the end of O'Connor's "Revelation," self-righteous Mrs. Turpin also has this revelatory vision of all things being made new. But the revelation for her is far from pleasant, because underneath her vision of the last being first — the poor white trash and the "niggers" — is the promise of judgment.

And just so in the book of Revelation. Following the vision where death will be no more comes a promise of the lake of fire for those who have fallen away. And so we are left with questions at the close of Scripture, questions about universal salvation and whether or not there are limits to God's mercy — unanswerable questions on this side of eternity. But these stories fill our imaginations and provide an opening for grace, fostering an underlying sense of hope against the alternative of despair. And like Pascal, like George Steiner and others, I place my wager — my bet — on merciful Transcendence.

Transformation of the Imagination
and Responsible Engagement

All good literature, like all good art in general, opens up the imagination, where, by the grace of God, the mysterious Ineffable shines through and we glimpse some truth to live by. As previously noted, good art begins with the world at hand, but does not rest there. It creates an opening onto transcendent possibility.

However, as we have considered here, contemporary writers create out of their culture, playing with the cards they are dealt. And for the most part, that deck is stacked with individualistic, materialistic, amoral cards. Contemporary stories mostly don't deal with religious experience of any kind — from mystical to practical — or if they do, the religious character is portrayed as a cultic nut or a fool.

But there are exceptions, some of which we have looked at here. Exceptions where God is hinted at, where divine Presence haunts the background of a work, where matters that matter — issues of love, mercy, death, and hope — are portrayed in such a way that the engaged viewer opens onto a world with the power to transform his or her life. (For example, after reading *Dead Man Walking,* I became quite active in working for a death-penalty moratorium in this country.)

The imagination has the power to transform vision, and it is a power for good or evil. It is a power of the human mind that can open onto the diabolic as well as the ineffable Other. In large part we become what we read and what we see and what we take into our imaginations. That is why a novel like Dan Brown's *The Da Vinci Code* or a movie like Mel Gibson's *The Passion of the Christ* stirs up so much controversy. These creative works hit people at the core of their imaginative consciousness, at the source of their faith.

So again the conclusion here is that you and I must make choices about what we feed our imaginations, because our imaginations shape our world. We make our choices from within a world that is given to us, as well as a world that can be imagined and chosen. And because our meeting with Transcendence requires an openness to creative intuition and divine grace, an opening onto the possible, then in addition to novels and plays, which typically demand some kind of closure, we might expand our reading to include more open-ended genres — fantasy, myth, poetry, even some children's stories (like C. S. Lewis's Narnia series or Martin Bell's short story "Barrington Bunny" — a delightful tale about life-giving love), stories that are fit for adults. Such myths, fairy tales, and "wonder stories" (such as tales by Chaim Potok) are marvelously rich fare for our imaginative flights toward God. Such literature offers us an intuition of the sacred, an opening onto the holy, coloring our inner worlds and deepening our grasp of what might very well be true.

Perhaps in the end, the writing and reading or viewing of fiction *and* the life of faith both involve paying attention, page by page, as the story unfolds. "Day by day, year by year, your own story unfolds, your life's story," Frederick Buechner says. "Things happen. People come and go. The scene shifts. Time runs by, runs out."[41] If fiction — all fiction, sacred or secular — helps us pay attention to meaning and what it means to be truly human — made in God's image — then it is religious fiction. Buechner comments, "If it is God we are looking for, as I suspect we all of us are even if we don't think of it that way and wouldn't use such language on a bet, maybe the reason we haven't found him is that we are not looking in the right places."[42]

In this chapter we have looked and paid attention in some "right places," some places of sacred and secular story that open our imaginations onto the Divine. We have met God here and there in story. We have caught glimmers of Transcendence through these imaginative works, glimmers which tell us that all is not dark, and beyond the dark is light and hope.

41. Frederick Buechner, *Secrets in the Dark* (San Francisco: HarperSanFrancisco, 2006), pp. 182-83.
42. Buechner, *Secrets in the Dark,* p. 183.

Coda: Criteria for Truth

Revelation is divine or transcendent disclosure of God's self to humans. I have proposed that the primary human locus of such disclosure is the imagination, which intuits God's impingement on consciousness and in turn creates a world of meaning by way of ritual movement, music, poetry, and stories. Thus, those who create literary and other forms of imaginative art reveal their glimpses of Transcendence to others who engage with them, through dialogue, in a process of co-creation, a development and sharing of meaning in community. This background sense or vision of what is real gives depth, purpose, and direction to our lives.

Across all the chapters thus far we have examined the imagination as a conduit for revelation — through direct mystical experience (introduction), through bodily ritual and the experience of music in community (Chapter One), through poetic and visual art (Chapter Two), and finally through the story told (Chapter Three). The point again is that it is the imaginative power (the God-given way in which humans are hardwired) that provides the locus for transcendent, revelatory truth to be revealed. Through imagination's gateway, divine truth and human truth intersect. If that gateway is open, we can flourish and be transformed in the process.

But here is the troubling question. How do we know that what we have glimpsed in a poem or work of art, or experienced firsthand in meditative prayer or ritual, or seen glinting in a short story by O'Connor or seen depicted in a film by Scorsese — how do we know that what we have glimpsed and formed in our imagination is true? What if what glitters on the edges of the story is not real gold but only fool's gold?

You see, once we focus on the imaginative power of the individual reader of story or the individual viewer of art, once we concentrate on an individual's or even a community's imaginative response to a work of art or literature, sacred or secular, then we reduce, for example, the objective authority of the church's teaching. Once we concentrate on our imaginative response to the stories contained in Scripture — as literary art also having revelatory power (albeit of a special warrant, as we saw in Chapter Three) — then we also reduce the objective authority of the scriptural word. And there is some risk entailed in the process.

Of course, there never has been any unmediated reading of Scripture, never has been a time — given the nature of human consciousness — when the Hebrew and Christian scriptures were not read through the lenses of culture and historical periods. Nevertheless, there is a tradition of interpretation for scriptural texts, and certainly there is a historical core to Judeo-Christian religion; both are real and need to be taken into account. As I have maintained throughout this text thus far, such historical data and traditional teachings and liturgical forms supply the necessary parameters, the grounding for our imaginative products. Tradition in general roots our imaginative power within the wisdom of the faith community. Imagination, as such, is neither good nor evil, but it has the power to run amok or even generate evil ideation if left unmoored within the larger picture of God's story.

And yet, there has to be room for ongoing revelation, for inspiration, intuition, and openness to divine breath — inspiring our own consciousness and the life of the larger community. Otherwise, as I have said before, tradition hardens into a dead place of rote, lifeless mouthings and leaden practice.

But again, how do we know that what we have glimpsed is from God? How do we know that we have met God or experienced some glimpse of spiritual truth or core meaning about human existence within our creative imagination? In part by using certain criteria — and at this juncture I would like to suggest five criteria for judging the truth value of our images and our imaginings. The following discussion of the criteria has a Christian flavor to it, but I believe that these principles hold for other faith traditions as well.[1]

---

1. For this discussion I have drawn primarily from David Brown's *Discipleship and Imagination: Christian Tradition and Truth* (New York: Oxford University Press, 2000).

Historical Criteria

For Judeo-Christian belief, there are a few certain historical occurrences, manifestations of God's work in our own history, that are of the essence, and without these occurrences, the religious system itself would make no sense. Of core significance for Christianity is obviously the birth, death, and resurrection of Jesus Christ at a certain time and place in world history. Paul says, "If Christ did not rise from the dead, your faith is in vain."

There are certain essential, decisive events for the believer that no amount of imaginative spinning can eliminate without doing central violence to the whole traditional belief system. Not that this hasn't occurred in the past, but such imaginings have been considered heterodox, outside the pale of world meaning for the Christian believer.

Thus, these historical criteria are a first criterion for truth generated by imaginative insight, of a first but not of a final significance. Not final, because metaphorical truth can stand, even if some non-essential historical facts of the matter turn out to evaporate into mere legend. For example, in the story of Jonah, it is unlikely that this prophet was ever swallowed by a fish, lived three days in its belly, and then was spat out in order to go prophesy to the Ninevites. However, the truth of that story remains: God's care is universal, and even those who were not Israelites, if repentant, were saved by God. The Bible is replete with such imaginative stories that we know are not literally, historically true but that convey deep truth nonetheless.

Empirical and Moral Criteria

Human reason has contributed not only to scientific knowledge but also to the cultural, moral development shedding light on interpersonal dealings and individual rights based on human dignity. Thus, over the centuries we have come to appreciate — at least in the Western mind — certain facts about human beings. For example, we have come to understand that gender differences are irrelevant before the law, and that there are no essential differences in terms of human worth between the sexes. We have also come to appreciate — over the past hundred years, in any case — that children, as well as women, are not chattel. We have come to understand that all races and peoples have equal value in the eyes of God and man.

We will not find unambiguous narrative, poetic, or legal warrant for these images in Scripture. But in terms of our own imaginings, our own background worldviews, our own imaginative perception of reality, these intuitions and concepts held in consciousness and conscience and hence law are fundamental. Therefore, an imaginative generation of a worldview that projects otherwise — an imaginative world created by the Nazis or by the Taliban, for example — would be considered false.

Ecclesial Criteria

The Bible is primarily the church's book, and the church, as a conservative watch-guard of orthodox belief, is charged with safeguarding the faith for future generations. Thus, one test for truth value of images and visions arising from creative engagement with stories and art is whether they pass muster with ecclesiastical oversight. That being said, in *Discipleship and Imagination* David Brown points out in his discussion of this truth criterion that conflict between individuals and church factions can be fruitful in ferreting out the truth of a matter. Ideas get thrashed out in controversy, and truth gets winnowed from falsehood in the dialectic of debate. For example, many hope, in the current controversy over human sexuality (based on very different worldviews coming from very different understandings of scriptural and theological images and concepts of human being within God's story), that from such conflict we will finally sift out the truth of the matter — at least as best we can in our finite understandings of God's ways.

It is my position here that the imagination gives us access to Transcendence, and this promise also holds true for the church as an ecclesial whole. The church in general holds a communally shared, imaginative vision based on a dynamically developing tradition rooted in history, symbol, and myth. Thus, as Brown asserts, no official pronouncements of the church can guarantee truth any more than Scripture itself can. But the corporate church does protect against individual arrogance and prejudice (and imaginative spinnings that undergird both). And God's Spirit remains active throughout the entire body of the faithful. As believers, we hope that truth can be found somewhere within the body of the church.

Criteria of Imaginative Engagement

In the introduction and these first three chapters I've made the case that rituals, music, liturgy, poems, visual art, and stories, in all their various presentations, can have a transformative effect on our imaginations, coloring our whole world of experience: creating profound meaning in our life, showing us what it means to be human beings, why we are here, what is our ultimate destiny. Certain imaginative products with which we engage have a substantial impact on our entire lives. Legends of Mary Magdalene as a sinner-saint, of Joan of Arc as a brave visionary, and of the lives of many saints have been potent in changing lives. How many have been drawn to the legend of St. Francis of Assisi — how many lives have been shaped by this image of the itinerant preacher of poverty and God's creative goodness?

Thus, one important criterion for truth is the way the image engages us. Brown refers to the "worked through example," explaining that we "often have to see something lived through before we can form a realistic estimate of its truth, and the writer of fiction helps us to see such a possible life in the round."[2]

Imaginative engagement with sacred themes continued to occur well after the close of the biblical canon and has continued over time down to this day. Just as the biblical narratives, much of them fictionalized history, laid claim to truth embedded in metaphor, symbol, allegory, analogue, and story, just so can truth be continually, imaginatively uncovered by engagement with stories today.

Criteria of Traditional Continuity

Finally, a test for validity of imaginary insight rests on the continuity between the intuition and resulting concept and the historical trajectory linking earlier with later visions. To take an example from our last

2. Brown, *Discipleship and Imagination*, p. 403.

chapter: in Martin Scorsese's *Last Temptation of Christ*, the image of Jesus arising from that film's story is one of human frailty — anxiety, doubt, and temptation. But in questioning the validity of this image, one could ask about the continuity with our traditional understanding — in one sense — of the human side of the Christ. Perfect God, yes, but also perfect man, according to the ancient creeds. Since the nineteenth century, there has been an increasing emphasis on Jesus' humanity, and even though you might reject aspects of Scorsese's portrayal, it does show continuity with tradition, both within Scripture and beyond Scripture over time, which would perhaps allow it some validity.

For Brown and for us, the imagination's role is central to our faith and our tradition, the imaginative "motor that has ensured the continuous adaptation of God's revelation to the world under new circumstances and conditions."[3] As Brown points out, this whole human/divine process is a messy one, entailing God's deep involvement with folks like you and me, a "fallible Bible and a fallible Church interacting with a no less fallible wider world."[4] Discipleship is about a continuing process of transformation, and our still developing, imaginative-based tradition is at the heart of our belief.

3. Brown, *Discipleship and Imagination*, p. 405.
4. Brown, *Discipleship and Imagination*, p. 405.

SECTION II

The Development
of the Imaginative Mind

Imagining is perhaps as close as humans get to creating some-
thing out of nothing the way God is said to. It is a power that to
one degree or another everybody has or can develop, like whis-
tling. Like muscles, it can be strengthened through practice and
exercise.

Frederick Buechner,
Whistling in the Dark[1]

The power of the imagination is not to be underestimated. Witness this
testimony:

> I believe that I found God/God found me through the experience of
> my imagination. Three years ago when I was in a really lonely place,
> . . . I was determined to find a way to nurture my soul because it had
> been so wounded. I didn't want to depend on other people; I wanted
> to find something that I could dig inside and find. What I discovered
> was that I could immerse myself in my photography. I came to realize
> a peace that was different than anything I'd known. Time would take
> on an altered quality, and my interior world was filled with
> magic. . . . It didn't take long [for me] to realize that when I looked

1. Frederick Buechner, *Whistling in the Dark* (San Francisco: HarperSanFrancisco,
1993), p. 69.

through my camera, I was finding God. I was moving in a direction that led me to Christianity. . . . I feel that when I play my violin, photograph, knit, cook, write — do any of the imaginative activities I love — I am reaching toward (and sometimes connecting with) God.

This was written by a former parishioner of mine at a church where I was rector. It is part of a handwritten note given to me about four years before I began to write this book. I happened across it as I was cleaning out a closet recently, and I was struck by its insight. I believe it captures what I now want to consider. Our capacity to imagine the unseen, our power to create a new world vision for ourselves, our ability to transcend the concrete given and envision a future filled with hope and promise — these lie at the core of religious faith and its development.

But what exactly is this capacity that we have circled around for a hundred pages or so? A little reflection will show that I've used the term *imagination* in at least two ways. First, I've focused on the capacity itself, considering it as a God-given power to create and co-create with others, through symbols (gesture, metaphor, sound, image, story), new worlds of meaning. Second, I've also considered this power in turn as shaped by life experience, as vital or dormant, a gateway open or relatively closed to new experience as in part a consequence of our backgrounds. Perhaps the best way to sum up the way I've conceived of imagination here is to say that the imaginative power is both *given* as part of our human equipment and thus can be a conduit for God's presence and grace, and *shaped* by various means — for example, by the books we read, the movies we see, the conversations we have with significant others.

We are concerned here with the imagination that matters, with that capacity which opens us up to Transcendence and which can be enhanced through life experience. Do we need to be concerned then with individual differences in imaginative power that may in part be genetically influenced? William James said, "Some persons . . . are incapable of imaging the invisible."[2] Is this true?

I actually don't think it is. Oh yes, some folks are more "imaginative" than others. We all know that. We say our friend Susie has a rich

---

2. William James, *Varieties of Religious Experience,* centenary edition (New York: Routledge, 2002), p. 292.

imagination because she weaves stories that entertain us at cocktail parties and dresses with flair and a little whimsy. But on the other hand, Tom is so boring, with his endless prattle about crabgrass and balky lawnmowers and the latest cute thing his two-year-old did with her breakfast cereal. Never get caught having lunch with Tom!

But could Tom have developed richer imaginative skills with a different childhood shaping, with parents who encouraged his fantasy life, with a house filled with books of poetry and paintings? Could he *now* develop a richer imaginative life by attending a workshop on poetry appreciation and joining a drama club? Or, to ask the age-old question all over again here, how much of our creative, imaginative capacity is contributed by nature, and how much by nurture?

It probably is the case that true imaginative geniuses, those uppermost "outliers" on the bell curve of creative intelligence such as Mozart and Einstein, inherited some particular gene or set of genes that gave them special creative power with music or mathematics and thus set them apart from the herd. But what about the rest of us huddled under the great middle bulge of that bell curve? How much of this imaginative creativity is contributed by nature (and thus hardwired, "no refunds and no exchanges") and how much by nurture?[3]

The answer, of course, is finally indeterminable in quantitative terms, and qualitatively, the answer is that both nature and nurture matter for each one of us. Thus, this dichotomy for all practical purposes has always been illusory, since nurture has pretty much always interacted with nature. Certainly some unknown percentage of the differences observed between people's creative abilities is inborn. But since genetic engineering with the aim of creating some super-race of Mozarts is ethically suspect, you do what you can on the nurture side of things, you do what you can with what you've got. And as we will see in this section, the most important elements of nurture that stimulate and enrich our creative imaginations occur in childhood and adolescence.

In fact, differences in creative ability in children can be seen as

3. Natalie Angier describes the latter as "that glorious conceptual duffel bag into which we stuff soft things like how you were treated by your parents, peers, and the parish priest; whether anybody bothered to hang a sixty-five-dollar Lamaze mobile over your crib; and whether you spent your childhood summers canoeing in the Adirondacks or sampling paint chips from the floor of your Bronx apartment." From "Do Straw Men Have DNA?" *American Scholar* 72, no. 2 (Spring 2003), p. 130.

young as three years of age, with those shown to be more imaginative having parents who encourage a rich fantasy life (e.g., engaging in pretend play with their children, expressing delight in their children's fantasy and imaginative play, reading to them from an early age). Children whose parents acknowledge and "collude" with them when they invent imaginary playmates also tend to be creative in later life.

In short, early opportunities for make-believe play are likely very important in facilitating the development of imaginative thought. As Jerome Singer explains, *"Imaginative play lays the foundation for a fundamental human capacity of lifelong value — the capacity for thinking about the possible, for wondering 'might this be?'* The ability to transform objects or settings into possible alternatives is crucial for adult thought, planning, and creativity."[4] But despite the fact that childhood and youth factors are very important for the development of our imaginative ability, possibilities for adult enrichment exist that can stir the most pedestrian of imaginative minds, and we shall look at some of these in this section.

In some sense, this second section of the book is the culmination of our discussion in the first section. If our capacity to imagine were fixed at birth, hardwired genetically like the color of our eyes or hair, then there would have been no need for this discussion. Why lay out an argument for the central importance of the imagination for faith development if some have the capacity and some simply do not?

But again, that is not the premise here. The premise here is that all of us, more or less, possess a creative, imaginative faculty that not only allows us to organize and make sense of incoming stimuli (Coleridge's primary imagination), but also allows us to remember, hope, and project an as-yet-unrealized world of meaning (Coleridge's secondary imagination), based on our experience but going beyond it. All of us can form images, more or less, of what we're not experiencing at the moment but what we might experience next week or next year or in the next life; we can all imaginatively recall what we have experienced last month or last year or imagine what we would like to experience as ideal.

And much if not all of our imagining has an emotional component

---

4. Jerome Singer, quoted in Jeffrey Goldstein's *Toys, Play, and Child Development* (New York: Cambridge University Press, 1994), p. 3, emphasis added.

to it, whether satisfying, joyful, or sometimes fearful — an aesthetic dimension — a kind of "emotional intelligence."[5] And like other aspects of our human intelligence, this imaginative aspect — across the life span, from early childhood to the end of life — needs educating, shaping, nourishing, and enriching. That is the subject we turn to in this section. My working assumption here is this: If we conceive of the imagination as a power or capacity we all possess at least in nascent form, then analogous to a virtue such as patience, it becomes strengthened through practice.

And so here we will examine various practices by which our imaginative capacity is exercised and expressed, nourished, and enriched. This will not by any means be an exhaustive examination. Instead, I will select examples of practices for children, youth, and adults, both in the home and in the community and churches, that can enhance the creative imagination. (The appendix will provide a list of resources for those wishing to nourish their own or their children's creative powers.) I am not going to make a hard distinction between sacred and secular spheres of influence, because our primary focus here is on the imagination as a power that can be enhanced and nurtured across these domains.

I want to focus on practices expressed through the imaginative categories associated with transcendent experience that we have already explored in detail in the first section — ritual and music, poetry and visual art, story and myth, as well as various prayer practices. I'm going to consider these particular categories of imaginative expression because rationally our imagination, which is active in creating a meaningful religious horizon and which is open to transcendent meaning, is touched more closely by the poetic and the aesthetic than by the mathematical and the technical.

At least this is my bias. I'm sure that a mathematician who swoons over an exquisite mathematical proof, or an engineer who grows ecstatic over a bridge design, or, for that matter, the inventor of an "ergonomically correct snow shovel," would argue with me. And many contemporary scholars have made the argument for the convergence of science and religion (e.g., both fields reach beyond the observable, describing reality in terms of metaphors and models). Nevertheless, here

---

5. Daniel Goleman, *Emotional Intelligence: Why It Can Matter More than I.Q.* (New York: Bantam Books, 1995).

I'm concerned with the evidence for faith experience and imaginative expression associated with what seems to lie closer to poetry and music than mathematical terms.

Further, because the literature suggests that specific nurture in childhood is vital for the development of a lively imagination, much of the discussion will center on practices within families and communities that seem to foster imagination and creativity in our youth. But I will also include spiritual and aesthetic practices for adults that enhance relevant imaginative expression, such as creating poetry circles, joining storytelling workshops, and using various prayer techniques that employ imagery.

CHAPTER FOUR

Exercising the Imagination:
Practices in the Home

Religion, like charity, begins at home. The daily round of family activities must somehow be brought into the presence of God. Parents praying, families eating together, conversations focusing on what is proper and improper, and sacred artifacts are all important ways in which family space is sacralized.

Robert Wuthnow, *Growing Up Religious*[1]

In the late 1990s, Mihaly Csikszentmihalyi undertook a study at the University of Chicago that examined the background characteristics of very creative people, exceptional folks who had a proven track record of substantial contribution to our culture — people like the pediatrician and later peace activist Benjamin Spock, the sitar artist Ravi Shankar, the biologist Jonas Salk, the poet Denise Levertov (whom we met earlier in this book), and the jazz pianist Oscar Peterson. Csikszentmihalyi started from the premise that all of us are born with two tendencies: a tendency toward conservation of energy, or an inclination to play it safe, to protect ourselves from risk and harm; and a tendency to explore, to take risks, to discover, to create, to venture forth into unknown waters.[2]

---

1. Robert Wuthnow, *Growing Up Religious: Christians and Jews and Their Journeys of Faith* (Boston: Beacon Press, 1999), p. 8.

2. Mihaly Csikszentmihalyi, *Creativity* (New York: HarperCollins, 1997).

Csikszentmihalyi assumed that this latter tendency toward creative, imaginative discovery, which we all inherit by virtue of being human, can vanish or at least erode if conditions are present that snuff it out. When the risk is too great, when there is no access to cultural artifacts such as books and art that provide our culture's building blocks for new creation, when there are no imaginative models or encouragement in the environment, when, for whatever reason, all one's energy is spent in just getting by from one day to the next, this creative tendency can simply decay.

So Csikszentmihalyi began with those who had taken the risk of creation and discovery, and he interviewed them in late adulthood in order to discover background factors that might have laid the foundation for their life's imaginative work. Because these were exceptional people (although really no Mozarts in the sample), a genetic predisposition toward science or an artistic bent — inborn talents as such — likely played an important role. But it also became apparent that environmental nurture counted too.

Many of Csikszentmihalyi's findings were obvious. That is, most (but not all) of these creative folks were born into homes with "cultural capital" — that is, as children they were often surrounded by interesting books, stimulating conversations, parental and peer expectations for success of some kind, imaginative role models, and teachers who noticed them, cared about them, and challenged them.

But Csikszentmihalyi also made the point that neither genes nor early childhood environment was entirely determinative of creative, imaginative potential in adulthood. At least a few in his sample came from poor homes and impoverished backgrounds. The most fundamental factors that seemed to account for living an imaginative life were inner energy and time available to ask questions and pursue the risk of discovery. Conversely, internal obstacles included "selfish goals, self-preservation, and fear of risk." Exhaustion, distraction, and laziness — giving in to entropy — were also pretty high on the list of obstacles for imaginative creativity.

Those with both energy and discipline, who took time to rest and to play as well as work, who stayed grounded in a tradition and mastered a discipline, but who also sometimes broke out beyond the molds of that tradition, who breached the bounds of their known domain and ventured into the margins of new territory, these turned out to have lived imaginative lives. "As they moved along in time, being bombarded by external events, encountering good people and bad, good breaks and bad, they had to make do with whatever came to hand. Instead of being shaped by events, they shaped events to suit their purposes."[3]

This study was not particularly concerned with factors that fostered the imagination as an opening onto Transcendence, and so Csikszentmihalyi gave little attention to religious faith per se. Those who were religious early in life remained strong believers to the end. But there were few conversions to religious orthodoxy in this sample of imaginative and gifted elders who were approaching the end of their lives. However, Csikszentmihalyi also found that even with those creative souls who had never embraced a "ritualized faith," what he termed a *broader faith* seemed to be much in evidence at the end of life — "a faith in an ultimately meaningful universe, which imposes requirements of awe and respect . . . on men and women. . . . We reach [a certainty], in the most private fibers of our being, that our existence is linked in a meaningful way with the rest of the universe."[4] In the end, their imaginations opened out onto some sense of Transcendence — for most of them nonpersonal, but nevertheless real.

This study and many others have shown clearly that a rich, imaginative life is rooted deeply, although not entirely, in the home of one's childhood and youth. Accordingly I'll turn first to some examples of practices in the home that nourish and enrich our imaginative capacity to reach beyond the mundane tasks of our daily living to encounter a transcendent Other through grace-filled engagement.

Rituals in the Home

We find the exercise of our imagination through ritual expression everywhere — in our daily home life, in our schools and public meetingplaces, and of course, in our churches' and synagogues' liturgical practices. In this section I'll concentrate on examples of imaginative ritual practices in the home that exercise and educate the aesthetic imagination.

Catherine Wallace tells a delightful story of how, when she was a

---

3. Csikszentmihalyi, *Creativity,* p. 181.
4. Csikszentmihalyi, *Creativity,* pp. 229, 233.

child, her mother always baked three loaves of bread at a time, and then asked her to walk out into the evening darkness, clutching a loaf, delivering it to one of the neighbors in need. At the time, this duty might have seemed onerous. But the practice — within her family a ritualistic habit with an embedded communal meaning of neighborliness and hospitality — ingrained in her a sense of generosity and a moral ethic, a habit that in part has likely helped shape her sense of shared community in adulthood.[5]

Thus, this ritual that Wallace practiced in her childhood home was not just a habitual pattern of behavior, but was linked to, and shaped by, stories of hospitality and generosity embedded in Bible and culture. Her cold walks out on winter nights to deliver that loaf of bread tucked under her coat were given meaning, even if perhaps not articulated at the time, by the images, metaphors, and parables she had absorbed as a child growing up in an Irish Catholic family.

In Chapter One I talked at length about the symbolic value of ritual, and here we would do well to remind ourselves of the profound significance of expressed bodily meaning. Ritualized actions are imaginative and interpretive acts through which we express meaning in our lives. They convey culturally shaped expressions with shared social meaning. (Otherwise they would be strictly idiosyncratic, having no communicative value within our communal life.) Our rituals are informed by the stories we share, and our narratives are given expression and enfleshed through symbolic behavior. As Herbert Anderson and Edward Foley explain, "In our rituals, like our stories, we narrate our existence, . . . we individually and collectively express and create a vision of life."[6] And it is our imagination that "blends" our bodily expression with the meaning given and shaped by our community's stories, culture, and history. Through ritual actions we not only express culturally shared meaning but also create new meaning for ourselves with the potential to "alter our conceptions at a stroke."[7]

5. Catherine Wallace, "Storytelling, Doctrine, and Spiritual Formation," *Anglican Theological Review* 81, no. 1 (1999): 39-59.

6. Herbert Anderson and Edmund Foley, *Mighty Stories, Dangerous Rituals* (San Francisco: Jossey-Bass, 1998), p. 26.

7. Barbara Myerhoff, "Death in Due Time: Construction of Self and Culture in Ritual Drama," in *Readings in Ritual Studies,* ed. Ronald Grimes (Upper Saddle River, N.J.: Prentice Hall, 1996), p. 408.

If you were raised in a home that was in any sense "religious," then I'm sure what remains in your memory most vividly are the ritualistic practices that were woven into the fabric of your family life. Such rituals were often linked with daily acts of eating (eating Sabbath dinners), dressing (wearing special clothes for church or synagogue), and sleeping (praying with a parent at bedtime). Rituals were also connected with decorating the home, with Advent wreaths and Christmas trees or menorahs lit, with Easter eggs hidden, with icons or crucifixes or fonts of holy water by the door. On holidays and High Holy Days there were "rules" for the proper times for rising and gift-giving, and there were proper ingredients and recipes for food preparation and proper times for feasting handed down from parent to child, ritualistic observances that needed to be followed year after year.

Even if Christmas and Easter are not especially celebrated as religious holidays in the home, nevertheless the rituals associated with such holidays can supply a foundation for religious faith. For example, American children believe that Santa and the Easter Bunny and even the Tooth Fairy visit at night. And as one writer points out, night is for mystery and for the uncanny and the ineffable. There is a sense in our children, at any rate, that these iconic figures will come only "if you believe," which "requires children to accept an unseen reality without conditions of patent proof."[8] Perhaps this capacity, requiring the exercise of the child's imagination to accept, unseen, a mysterious reality and thus gain access to Transcendence, does contribute in some way to the foundation of religious faith.[9]

Karen-Marie Yust has written an excellent book that concretely details practices that will nourish children's imagination relevant to faith development, and I have relied heavily on that book for much of the discussion here. In a section titled "Expanding Awareness through Intuition and Bodily Knowledge," Yust details spiritual practices for children (along with their parents or other adult role models) that involve using the body in symbolic expression and meaning creation.[10]

She points out that actions speak louder than words to children. In

8. Cindy Dell Clark, *Flights of Fancy, Leaps of Faith* (Chicago: University of Chicago Press, 1995), p. 107.

9. Karl Rosengren, Carl Johnson, and Paul Harris, *Imagining the Impossible* (Cambridge: Cambridge University Press, 2000).

10. Karen-Marie Yust, *Real Kids, Real Faith* (San Francisco: Jossey-Bass, 2004).

a loving environment, children tend to imitate what they see grown-ups do. A two-year-old in a booster seat will observe a parent offering a blessing at dinner, and that nightly practice around the table will shape her childhood memories, becoming ingrained as embodied habit — even if it's something she doesn't actually do later in life. A five-year-old can help light an Advent wreath or a menorah candle, and such practices give meaning that becomes embedded in ritual form. "They watch us to see whether we bow our heads or raise our hands when we pray," Yust says; they notice that we kneel or make the sign of the cross, trying to imitate with their own gestures. "And in the doing, their bodies take on and grasp intuitively a sense of meaning created in the performance, informed, to be sure, by the stories and lessons we tell them."[11] Again, the sense of these rituals — the imaginative, intuitive "feel" for the Holy — remains ingrained in the adult psyche even if the specific religious teachings drop out along the way.

As this discussion is meant to be only illustrative, I'll focus on one ritual practice with variations on a patterned theme. Yust describes six prayer postures, each one eliciting within the body a different sense of reverence, with these senses arising both from inborn cues within the body (those orientation senses that our bodies possess from infancy and early childhood, discussed at length in Chapter One) and from the differential significance that various religious traditions give to these postures.

For example, kneeling gives rise to a sense of humility and penitence; lying prostrate signifies suffering and spiritual emptiness; bowing one's head connotes reverence. However, some prayer practices are more remote from our inborn sense of orientation. For example, for Christians, making the sign of the cross is a learned practice and a visible witness to the self and others that one worships one God in Triune form. Other forms of prayer posture have no religious significance in themselves, but take on a religious meaning when joined with prayer. For example, sitting is not normally a prayer posture. But a sitting posture takes on contemplative meaning in some traditions that follow the monastic practice of meditative prayer. Such a posture assumed during times of silent prayer practice signifies attunement and receptivity to transcendent encounter. Yust says,

11. Yust, *Real Kids, Real Faith,* p. 140.

We can help [our children] recognize that spiritual awareness, like spiritual experience, is multi-sensory and encourage them to develop spiritual beliefs and practices that are consistent with one another [i.e., letting the body reflect the act of praying and, through its own senses, help create and transform the prayer moment into a prayerful, grace-filled meeting]. . . . We may even discover that we are growing in spiritual awareness alongside them as we, too, become more attuned to what we believe and do, and why.[12]

Most ritualistic expressions have embodied meaning inherent in them unless done by absolute rote. For example, every morning when I get up, the first thing I do is light a kerosene lamp on the kitchen table (well, after I pour my first cup of coffee!). The other lights are turned down, so the lamp shines in the dimness of the room. This is my prized time not only to eat breakfast but to do my spiritual reading, to pray and meditate.

These actions have great meaning for me. They are part of my everyday ritual of opening the day and opening my imagination to God. But, on reflection, I'm not always as mindful of this ritual's significance as I could be. That is, the action of striking the match and lighting the lamp could very well be accompanied by a short prayer invoking God's presence and preparing my heart and mind for divine encounter in the next hour's reading and praying. This mindfulness would immeasurably deepen the ritual pattern of my morning. So being imaginatively attentive to what you are doing can help keep the ritual vital.

Barbara Biziou has written a book called *The Joys of Everyday Ritual* that is filled with suggestions for household rituals that can creatively expand not only our children's but our own worlds of meaning, enriching our imaginations in the process. For example, she suggests creating a ritual space for meditation and prayer, arranging a quiet corner with a shelf holding an icon or a candle or an incense burner. She also recommends keeping a book of sacred poetry or a Bible nearby — in its own sacred nook or book holder.

For Biziou, the elements of ritual include intention or purpose (knowing why you are carrying out the ritual), sequence (carrying out the ritual in a certain order that has a beginning and an end), sacred

---

12. Yust, *Real Kids, Real Faith,* p. 142.

space (imaginatively creating a condition — like my lighting of the morning lamp — that sets the time and space apart from the mundane), ingredients (using symbols of meaning), and personal significance (following a pattern of personal importance).[13] Just so, I light my morning lamp before prayer time to create a sense of sacred place that is very important for the proper beginning of my day. My breakfast table becomes my altar.

Meditative Prayer Practice and Poetry in the Home

Robert Wuthnow makes the point that the spiritual practices of adults as well as children are linked with our social relationships. For children, these relationships are first and foremost within the family. For adults, these social groupings are generally voluntarily chosen, but most often reflect some sense of traditional linkage or affinity with their own childhood practices. That is, spiritual practices are woven into lifelong journeys having continuity with the personal past. Sometimes adults who were raised in observant Christian homes become devout Buddhists. But more likely they find their way into Christian communities in a nostalgic search for the lost comforts of youth.

However, the spiritual practices that connect us through the gateway of our imagination to a sense of the sacred do not come naturally. That is, these practices take time and effort to carry out and to become habitual ways of life, ways of being and doing that give meaning to our days. It does require effort and discipline to engage in a regular prayer practice yourself, or to teach your child to pray. But the cost of *not* making the effort is high. The Sufi poet Rumi says, "When you quit meditating, the layers of rust eat into your soul-mirror. There's no sheen."[14]

Yust maintains that children as young as kindergarten age can learn a form of brief, meditative prayer. And those older than ten can practice periods of silent, contemplative prayer, as well as practice what's referred to as centering prayer or guided imagery. There are various versions of centering prayer, but all involve four basic steps: (1) preparing or choosing a sacred word or phrase that has some symbolic spiritual

13. Barbara Biziou, *The Joys of Everyday Ritual* (New York: St. Martin's Press, 2001).
14. Quoted in Robert Wuthnow, *Growing Up Religious,* p. 192.

meaning; (2) centering down or attuning to God's presence by repeating that word or phrase to remain anchored in attentive waiting; (3) dismissing distractions when they arise by gently moving back to that anchoring symbol; and (4) finally returning to a sense of the everyday world by focusing again on everyday space and mundane tasks at hand.[15]

Alternatively, for younger children as well as for adults who find the silence of centering prayer difficult to inhabit for long, meditative prayer provides a rich, imaginative opening for spiritual, transcendent experience. During periods of meditative prayer, an imaginative prompt — a poem, an artwork such as an icon or a cross, music (such as a chant), or a visualized scene from Scripture — is used to open up a possible encounter with the Sacred.

There are wonderful resources even for young children that use poetry and guided imagery to stimulate their imaginations and open up transcendent meaning in their lives. One example is Shel Silverstein's *Where the Sidewalk Ends* — a book of humorous poetry that addresses serious spiritual and existential questions. A child as young as four or five can listen to such a poem, picture the poem in their heads while listening (a CD comes with the book), and maybe draw a picture in response. A second example using guided imagery is Sandy Sasso's *God's Paintbrush,* an interfaith book for children in which the author takes the child on an imaginative journey examining God's work in creation. On each beautifully illustrated page is an image of God's work in creation, followed by questions the child is to ponder imaginatively. For example, "Sometimes I imagine that when it gets very dark at night, the flowers, trees, mountains, and oceans are afraid. I wonder if God made the stars for them to go to bed with and the moon to be their night light? *When are you afraid? What makes you feel better?*"[16] Of course, these kinds of imaginative prayer practices can, with some adaptation, be used by adults too.

As I have discussed at length in this book, the creative artist brings to her work her background of personal experience, shaped and colored by a shared cultural world of meaning. These background experiences provide a fund of symbols and images that the artist's imagina-

---

15. Yust, *Real Kids, Real Faith,* p. 113.
16. Sandy Sasso, *God's Paintbrush* (Woodstock, Vt.: Jewish Lights Publishing, 1992).

tion can then reshape into new forms. Through such symbols and metaphors, the artist (visual artist, writer, sculptor, poet) penetrates beneath the everyday surface of things to provide signs or glimmers of Transcendence or divine penetration and indwelling in everyday life. The individual responding to the artwork, in engaging with and contemplating the symbols and metaphors, co-creates new meanings for himself or herself, and opens up the possibility of divine meeting in the process.

And so poetry for all age groups can act as an imaginative conduit — a gateway for divine impingement, for engagement with transcendent, spiritual reality. And there are wonderful resources to exercise the imagination along these lines. For example, Peggy Rosenthal, in her *Praying the Gospels through Poetry,* sees the reading of a poem as a "walk."[17] So first she quotes a Bible scene (the foot-washing of the Last Supper in John 13:1-15);[18] then she follows with a poem imaginatively engaging the story (in this case, George Herbert's poem "Love" — "Love bade me welcome; yet my soul drew back, guilty of dust and sin . . ."). She follows this with a "walk-through" of the poem, verse by verse. Finally, Rosenthal closes with questions for imaginative meditation.

Many of us shy away from reading poetry because it seems foreign, like a language with its own syntax and rhythm, its own notations and forms that make the whole practice appear somewhat esoteric and daunting.[19] One writer notes that while it seems relatively easy to fish and eat and hunt and mate, to earn a living and build houses and conquer territory, it is much more difficult to learn things that developed more recently in our cultural evolution — things like manipulating symbolic mathematical systems and reading and writing poetry.[20]

---

17. Peggy Rosenthal, *Praying the Gospels through Poetry* (Cincinnati: St. Anthony Messenger Press, 2001).

18. Rosenthal comments that "imagining a biblical scene more fully than Scripture details it has a long and rich heritage. Our best term for it is *midrash,* the Hebrew name for the age-old practice of rabbis commenting on a biblical passage by responding to it imaginatively" (*Praying the Gospels through Poetry,* p. 19).

19. Jill Pelaez Baumgaertner, "Hints of Redemption," *Christian Century,* 21 February 2006, p. 38. Also see her essay, "Silver Catching Midday Sun: Poetry and the Beauty of God," in *The Beauty of God: Theology and the Arts,* ed. Daniel J. Trier et al. (Downers Grove, Ill.: InterVarsity Press, 2007).

20. Csikszentmihalyi, *Creativity,* p. 125.

But it is possible to learn how to walk that path, and what an imaginative, joy-filled journey it can be — creative as we engage with rich symbols and metaphors — an imaginative meeting place where the deep truth of our human lives and the deep truth of reality intersect.

One of the best practical resources I have come across for reading poetry is a short book by Molly Peacock titled *How to Read a Poem . . . and Start a Poetry Circle.*[21] She apparently travels all over Canada and the United States, giving workshops on starting poetry circles, groups of various sizes that periodically meet to poke and prod poems for their deep meaning. The groups gather in private homes or public spaces such as libraries and bookshops.

Peacock says there are basically three rules for starting a poetry circle. First, start small — three or four people are enough for a lively discussion. Second, share responsibility. If you meet in each other's homes, rotate among them, and do whatever is necessary to make the meetings burden-free — for example, order pizza if you meet over dinner. Alternatively, have breakfast meetings at a local restaurant so no one is burdened with hosting. And third, limit the frequency of meetings. Make them monthly or quarterly — again so that they are pleasantly anticipated and not dreaded as burdens. I will select one delicious quote from Peacock that absolutely captures the spirit of her work:

> Conquering book lists, jostling for attention because you'd better look smart, slumping your shoulders because you feel so stupid, cooking for a crowd, cramming a schedule — all are out. All those things are inimical to poetry circles, which are divinely slow in a hurtling world, heavenly in their absence of social, philosophical, and psychological pressure, and best of all, *thrilling in their presence of revelation.*[22]

It is only in recent years that I have allowed myself to slow down and savor poetry as part of my meditative practice. Some of the poems that I have found revelatory I included in Chapter Two of this book. (I have included other resources in the Appendix.)

---

21. Molly Peacock, *How to Read a Poem . . . and Start a Poetry Circle* (Toronto: McClelland & Stewart, 1999).

22. Peacock, *How to Read a Poem,* pp. 201-2 (emphasis added).

Ignatian Spirituality and Gospel Imagery

I want to include at least a brief reference here to Ignatian spiritual exercises, an imaginative approach that combines the prayer practice of guided imagery and the meeting of God in the story proper. This practice is decidedly Christian in tone and content, but it will serve nicely as an example of a practice that situates the imagination at its core.

Ignatius of Loyola was a sixteenth-century Spanish soldier turned monk and priest who wrote the now-famous *Spiritual Exercises,* a series of teachings comprised of imaginative scriptural meditation, spiritual discernment, and prayer.[23] Ignatian prayer has become rather popular in recent years. It is a meditative practice that uses the imagination to visualize Gospel scenes embedded in biblical stories as well as to engage in imaginary dialogue with the divine Other. It is an excellent example of a prayer practice that specifically utilizes our imaginative capacity as the center of spiritual transformation.

Meditating on the *Exercises* can take the reader on a spiritual pilgrimage. The journey takes him or her through four stages aimed at creating a deeper opening with Transcendence: (1) imaginative meditations that confront the reader with his or her frailty and dependence on God; (2) imaginative visualization of Gospel scenes where Christ calls the "pilgrim" to Christian service; (3) imaginary engagement with scenes from the Passion of the cross, with emphasis on God's love for us and the world; and finally, (4) exercises that fill the imagination with Resurrection life, calling the pilgrim out into wholeness and love for others.[24]

Margaret Silf has written a text that would be useful as a kind of self-help vehicle for spiritual transformation. She takes an Ignatian approach to spiritual practice that the reader could carry out at home.[25] After describing three ways for the reader to enter the stories in the

23. See Ignatius of Loyola, *The Spiritual Exercises of St. Ignatius,* trans. Louis J. Puhl, S.J. (Westminster, Md.: Neuman Press, 1959); and Joseph Tetlow, S.J., *Ignatius Loyola: Spiritual Exercises* (New York: Crossroad, 1992). There is also an updated version aimed at being somewhat more palatable to modern minds: David Fleming, S.J., *Modern Spiritual Exercises* (New York: Image Books, 1983).

24. J. Robert Barth, *Romanticism and Transcendence* (Columbia: University of Missouri Press, 2003), p. 96.

25. Margaret Silf, *Companions of Christ: Ignatian Spirituality for Everyday Living* (Grand Rapids: William B. Eerdmans, 2005).

Gospels — imaginative meditation or "seeing" himself in the scene, "chewing over" the story, digesting its deepest significance for him, and focusing particularly on that aspect which catches and arrests his attention — Silf engagingly describes the transformation process.[26]

Although not everything we can imagine is necessarily true or good, if the fruit of your imaginative engagement with the text leaves you in a positive mood (brings joy and peace), if the images energize you rather than depress or dampen your spirit, then God is likely working on your soul, drawing you toward a new life. To paraphrase Silf, "Imagine yourself at age eighty. What will you wish you had done with your life?" When you reach the end of a day and review it, "Where did you feel most alive and touched by God's Spirit?"[27]

This brief look at Ignatian spirituality makes it clear that this is a practice where we use our imaginative power to envision and immerse ourselves deeply in the Gospel life, creating new future possibilities for personal transformation. I'll revisit this approach in the next chapter, which is concerned with creative practices in the community, because Ignatius's *Exercises* are most fruitfully taken up in the company of a spiritual soul friend or spiritual guide. Transformation is not merely a personal matter; the expression of a life well lived belongs finally to the community.

Stories Shared in the Home

We tell stories because our brains are hardwired to do so, because we are essentially narrative creatures, imaginatively retrieving memories of our past and projecting hopes for our future, creating the story of our lives. We imagine and tell our stories on a daily basis. In the evening I walk through the side door of the kitchen and exclaim to my husband,

---

26. Of course, these three ways are the same meditative practices applied to any story with potential spiritual weight. Nancy Malone says there are similarities that "silence, stillness, focused attention, and meditative reading share. We . . . think of meditation as an opportunity to reflect on our conversation with ourselves in the 'presence' of another, as we may do when we read. We might imagine God overhearing us, 'reading' us as we really are, good and bad, our naked selves." See *Walking a Literary Labyrinth* (New York: Riverhead Books, 2003), p. 135.

27. Silf, *Companions of Christ,* p. 61.

"Let me tell you about what happened to me when I walked into the front office!" And I spin my day's story out into an embodied dialogue of words and gestures.

As Catherine Wallace says, "It is an effort, a rich but weary effort, to make coherent sense of our own lives. And we know it is an effort, because we are doing it all the time, week after week, day after day: we work to make sense of our lives . . . [over] many cups of coffee . . . with sympathetic friends."[28] And because our lives are fragmented[29] and incomplete (after all, for most of us, the end is unknown, and thus our lives as they are being played out have a sense of incompleteness to them), we turn to scripted stories — biographies, novels, films, and plays — to satisfy our need for wholeness.

In reading or listening to a story, we are all co-creators with the teller, engaging in verbal or mental dialogue, self-transcending and being transformed in the process. As I discussed at length in Chapter Three of this work, we can imaginatively try on fictional identities in a relatively cost-free but potentially transforming way, tracing out in our imaginations the potential outcomes for various choices we might make along the way. And what we ultimately make of such engagement depends on imaginations rooted in a culture or tradition of meaning that shapes those images and hence finally shapes our lives.

Again, all of this is ground we've covered earlier in this work. But it bears emphasizing here that we have to make *choices* about what we fill our imaginations with and our children's imaginations with, because our imaginations and their products will shape our world of meaning. As Wallace says, "We belong to the stories that hold us, which are the stories that we hear from or with the people who matter to us the most."[30] We are at least as much what we read and hear as what we eat!

---

28. Wallace, "Storytelling, Doctrine, and Spiritual Formation," pp. 51-52.

29. I can't resist Wallace's colorful characterization of our fragmented days: "Real life is usually all too much like an incoherent, boring movie: miscellaneous disconnected events follow one another, but often what we have is no clear and self-evident sense of what is going on in our lives and why, or what's important and what's detail. Scene after scene muddles past, exactly like those days all of us know all too well in which we feel both terribly busy and entirely unproductive. If life in the ordinary weeks of our lives were a movie, most of us would probably hit 'rewind' and decide to go do some laundry instead." See "Storytelling, Doctrine, and Spiritual Formation," p. 51.

30. Wallace, "Storytelling, Doctrine, and Spiritual Formation," p. 41.

Reading with Children

We live and impart the life of faith to others through the stories we tell, which affirm that God is real, hope is possible, and life has ultimate meaning; that our frailties, our failures, our pains, and ultimately our deaths will not finally destroy us, but that ultimately all will be well in the end — our own end and the end of it all. The stories we tell are important not only to us but also to our children, as Wallace points out:

> If every night over dinner you tell your kids some story — even a very small and simple story — admiring some small bit of honesty or kindness you have seen that day, or maybe rejoicing in the chance you had to be kind or generous or straightforward, then your kids will grow up to be kinder, more honest, more generous, and more cheerful. If every night you complain about the evidence you have seen that people are just out for themselves and nobody can be trusted, your kids will grow up to be suspicious and distant. The stories we tell create the world.[31]

Even at a very young age, children are amazingly adept at absorbing stories and interweaving stories' characters into their own daily lives. Every child (and even those of us who are not so young) pleads, "Tell me a story," and a good story — a story that conveys a kernel of life-giving truth to us and to those we love — becomes a means of revelation.

Karen-Marie Yust's work is a treasure trove of practical ideas for faithful storytelling in the home. She lists four kinds of faith-filled storybooks: Bible-story books, books that imaginatively expand on Bible stories (employing the technique of *midrash,* creatively expanding and extending Bible stories), storybooks about other people and their lives that pick up on biblical themes, and books that contain stories about characters who express principles of godly living.[32]

Yust also gives many examples of such books that are readily available to purchase, rent, or borrow. (Community libraries as well as church libraries frequently have such books for loan.) Examples include Sandy Sasso's book *God's Paintbrush* (cited earlier) and her book *God in Between,* both of which raise questions "about what God is like and where

---

31. Wallace, "Storytelling, Doctrine, and Spiritual Formation," pp. 54-55.
32. Yust, *Real Kids, Real Faith,* p. 49.

God is to be found."[33] The story "Barrington Bunny," which I've cited earlier, is one of my personal favorites, depicting a life of self-sacrificing love, expressing metaphorically the life of Christ and Christian discipleship in a delightful, heartwarming tale.[34] These and other similar books can enrich bedtime routines with life-giving lessons rooted in a faith tradition. (References to selected works are given in the Appendix.)

Yust, building on earlier work by Walter Bruggemann, also describes important ways in which parents can actively engage children's own imaginations so that they retell sacred stories and thus make them their own. She suggests encouraging them to tell those stories in their own words, playing "a game in which we wonder together what some biblical character would look, sound, and act like if he or she live[d] in our neighborhood."[35] The importance of passing on sacred stories cannot be underestimated.

Imaginative Engagement with Stories

Novels, films, and plays, read or viewed in the company of others, can tap layers of deep human meaning in a way that is significant and potentially personally transforming. Nationally there seems to be a rise in book clubs for teens as well as adults — affinity groups that gather in living rooms and kitchens as well as in more public places such as bookstores, libraries, and coffeehouses. Some have given much of the credit for this phenomenon to Oprah Winfrey and her book recommendations, while others have linked this desire to gather and discuss life's great questions raised by fiction to the post-9/11 Zeitgeist. Whatever the root stimulus might be, most gatherings are primarily social, with private ones organized by friends who invite other friends. Bookstores are often willing to recommend selections. There are also Web sites provided by major publishers and newspapers, such as *The New York Times,* which provide book suggestions, along with readers' guides with discussion questions included.

33. Yust, *Real Kids, Real Faith,* p. 56.
34. "Barrington Bunny," in Martin Bell's *The Way of the Wolf* (New York: Walker & Company, 1984).
35. Yust, *Real Kids, Real Faith,* p. 65.

But again, if we are concerned with our imagination as a meeting place with God, if we are concerned with our imaginative power engaging with stories that can transform our lives and our children's lives in a positive spiritual direction, then we need to be selective in what we feed our souls. There are several dozen books labeled as "spiritual" on the market at any given time, but not all of them are rooted in the wisdom of a religious tradition.

Bridget Nichols, in her book *Literature in Christian Perspective,* supplies what she refers to as a "foundation library."[36] Her suggested library includes the Bible, of course, but also works of literature ranging from Shakespeare and Milton to contemporary novelists, such as Penelope Fitzgerald *(The Gate of Angels)*. Each chapter of Nichols's book is a self-contained study guide, with meditational questions that explore the deep meaning of specific works, facilitating the creation of meaning through the imaginative process.

Nichols sees the reader engaged in a two-way process of faith and reading. First, a reader's initial faith,[37] drawn from the sometimes tenuously planted roots of a religious tradition, nevertheless prompts the reading and informs to some extent the interpretation of the poem or story. Then the questions the reader asks, alone or in a group, engage the faith tradition in turn, casting a fresh slant on elements of belief.

When we read, we imaginatively engage in dialogue with the text of a story, creating fresh meaning perhaps unintended by the author. And when we read aloud to our child or spouse or best friend, that creates an intimacy that enlarges both of your worlds. I have known married couples who for years read aloud to one another, and I myself regularly engage in this wholly delightful shared activity. Nancy Malone eloquently describes the habit of reading at night:

> The night readings are quiet times that prepare us for sleep by making a break with other concerns. What this reading provides is a continuity to our lives that we share no matter what else is happening in "real" life. When things are somewhat scattered and hectic, the read-

36. Bridget Nichols, *Literature in Christian Perspective: Becoming Faithful Readers* (London: Darton, Longman & Todd, 2000).

37. Wallace defines faith as "a fundamentally imaginative act, as the creative capacity to perceive the Holy that permeates and sustains all the little gritty details otherwise known as 'the real world.'" See "Storytelling, Doctrine, and Spiritual Formation," p. 46.

ing calms us down physically and at the same time pulls us imaginatively and emotionally into African villages and nineteenth-century
French or Russian drawing rooms. . . . [This shared reading] vastly
extends the range of our human acquaintance, and at the same time
helps us accept the limits of the human condition.[38]

Finally, William Bausch gives a number of practical suggestions in
the area of spirituality and story. Some of them I will consider in the
next chapter. But two of them seem fitting for our discussion here. He
urges us both to contemplate the story and to pray the story. That is, he
suggests we apply the imaginative practices of imagery and prayer to
penetrate to the depths of the narratives — fiction and nonfiction —
that we read. He says, "In order to sense God working in our stories
[the ones we read, as well as the story of our lives], we must give time
to looking at them" — reflecting, chewing on their contents, digesting
their wisdom — in order to glimpse better "the patterns of grace and
sharpen our perception of the spirit."[39]

In Csikszentmihalyi's study of exceptionally creative people discussed at the beginning of this chapter, he reported a very interesting
finding. It turns out that when ordinary folks were signaled with an
electronic pager at different times of the day and asked to report how
creative they felt at that moment, they reported the highest levels of
imaginative, creative experience while they were walking, driving, or
swimming. In other words, they were most imaginatively creative when
they were engaged in a semi-automatic activity that required minimal
attention, which freed up mental energy that allowed them to make
connections with imaginative ideas lurking just below the surface of
their consciousness.

So perhaps one of the best places to exercise your imaginative
power and in the process to become more attuned to Transcendence
through imaginative engagement is to stroll out your front door, alone
or with a spouse or a child, and go for a walk in your neighborhood or
nearby garden or woods or urban zoo. Ponder a poem, or a scene from
a Gospel story, or an image from last night's novel that has haunted
you. For within the imagination resides the locus for meeting God.

38. Malone, *Walking a Literary Labyrinth,* pp. 126-27.
39. William Bausch, *Storytelling: Imagination and Faith* (Mystic, Conn.: Twenty-
Third Publications, 1995), p. 206.

CHAPTER FIVE

Exercising the Imagination:
Practices in Communities and Churches

Saul may have become Paul in the aloneness of religious ecstasy, but he could remain *Paul only in the context of the Christian community that recognized him as such and confirmed the "new being" in which he now located this identity. This relationship of [faith] and community is not a peculiarly Christian phenomenon. One cannot remain a Muslim outside the* 'umma *of Islam, a Buddhist outside the* sangha, *and probably not a Hindu anywhere outside India. Religion requires a religious community, and to live in a religious world requires affiliation with that community.*

Peter Berger and Thomas Luckmann,
The Social Construction of Reality[1]

At the beginning of this section I said that I wouldn't concentrate on the distinction between sacred and secular. If the Transcendent comes to us, impinges on us, through the imagination, then God speaks to us potentially through our engagement with all of creation. Thus, I have been most concerned here with practices which exercise and enhance that imaginative capacity, that power within us all to discover and create meaning beyond the concrete given.

But of course, context and culture do matter. What we imagina-

---

1. Peter Berger and Thomas Luckmann, *The Social Construction of Reality* (Garden City, N.Y.: Anchor Books, 1967), p. 158.

tively make of what we see, what we remember as important, and what we hope for in our future are shaped and colored by the symbols, language, and tradition of the various worlds they reflect. There is the everyday work world, the secular city we inhabit; and there is the world of religious traditions, which have their own special rituals, symbols, language, and overarching meaning.

For the religious person, the latter world of meaning shines its light on all of existence, the mundane as well as the sacred, and for many this overall grounding is rooted in practices of their childhood family. But for our purposes here, we will consider the contexts of community and church as distinct, and we will look at examples of practices within each context through which the imagination is exercised and strengthened.

Imaginative Practices within the Community

Ritualized practices symbolically expressing communal meaning are ubiquitous in our culture. We lower the American flag to half-mast to reflect a community-wide mourning. And the state-sponsored pomp that followed the recent deaths of both President Reagan and President Ford reflected through symbolic action the meaning of the high national office they both served. But beyond these sometimes grand public practices, rituals are created in our everyday lives as expressions of individual and group meaning.

Paul Willis, in his analysis of everyday creativity in what he terms our "common culture," assumes that the cultural products that become elements in the creative process are essentially consumer goods. And even though the work cited here was written nearly two decades ago, Willis's conclusions still seem at least culturally relevant. We live in a consumer culture, and so this is the world that provides opportunity for imaginative meaning-making. Willis persuasively argues that our youth are creative consumers, soaking in rap and pop music and then creating their own sounds on computerized mixers; wearing the latest jeans, but personalizing their look with flair; adorning their bodies with self-designed tattoos and piercings; and creatively making community in pubs and pick-up bands. By such imaginative means, Willis says, the youth in our communities fashion their own identity within a social matrix, living out their own sense of creative vitality in the process.[2]

But I think Willis's celebration of the consumer market as the arena for life's meaning-making is also a pretty limited view. It is my position here that our children and our youth, as well as you and I, who are probably well beyond those stages in life, inhabit potential worlds of meaning much deeper and larger than our consumer culture and its artifacts as we engage with the symbols and metaphors embedded in poetry, music, art, and story.

These various aesthetic domains differ in the ways that are best to engage them. That is, to experientially "know" Auden's poem "For the Time Being," we have to actually read it, preferably out loud. We can't know a piece of music by Bach by merely reading about it — we have to hear it. And we can't know God without some opening onto Transcendence, without prayer and conversation, without openness to image, symbol, and ritual conveying some sense of divine Presence.

Schools as Places for Imaginative Practices

Since the creative urge to make meaning in the face of life's deepest mysteries actually begins quite early in life, spaces as mundane as school playgrounds become places where some of life's basic questions can be creatively addressed.[3] Because this is not a book about education theory and practice, my examples of practices that enrich our youths' imaginations within the school setting are going to be few. But it should be obvious by now that if you're going to choose a school for your child, you would look very carefully at the curriculum. You would look for aspects of the school environment that would stimulate the imagination: Is poetry taught? Is there a music appreciation program, a school chorus or orchestra? Is visual art an essential part of the curriculum — not necessarily the making of art per se, but just as important, the appreciating of art in a creative process of engagement? Is creative writing emphasized? Are there fantasy books and music videos? Is

2. Paul Willis, *Common Culture* (Boulder, Colo.: Westview Press, 1990).

3. Ronald Cram, "Knowing God: Children, Play, and Paradox," *Religious Education* 91, no. 1 (1996): 55-73.

there free time for children to satisfy their curiosity and explore their interests? Is there unstructured playground time during which children can create songs and games whose images have been found to reflect their concerns, even deep concerns about life and death?[4] Is storytelling encouraged, with teachers as role models?[5]

John Bell, a musician and composer and a member of the ecumenical Iona community in Scotland, taught a group of Catholic musicians in Texas some songs from around the world. Five years later, Bell was invited to an elementary school in Austin to hear the results of his teaching. Bell heard the pupils sing songs in Zulu, Swahili, Yuribe, and Spanish. At that time he also found out that when the evening news included a story about South Africa, parents reported that these same children sang songs of that land. Clearly, the imaginative engagement of these children with the wider world of other cultures laid a foundation for empathy and mission beyond the borders of their own limited, local concerns. Bell says, "These children are growing up with an awareness of the world, and it's the song of the church which is making them aware of other cultures and of other people. Any school could do that — intertwine music with geography and history. . . ." Bell adds, ". . . and religious studies."[6] But in our culture, with its strict division of church and state, unless you place your child in a religiously affiliated school, the place for the latter is the church or synagogue and the home.

Once you find the right school environment, with all or at least some of the stimulating resources highlighted here, your child's imagi-

---

4. Cram, "Knowing God," pp. 58-63.

5. In her dissertation research, Nancy Wonder found that even youth from culturally deprived homes could be taught imaginative skills. In a sample of twelve- to fourteen-year-olds who had entered a delinquency prevention program, she initially found that they spent little time in imaginative activities. They lacked the environmental factors necessary for the development or enhancement of the imagination — namely, privacy, role models, and storytelling opportunities. After an eight-week intervention aimed at teaching them imaginative skills, most showed a significant increase in creative thinking, story content rich in detail, and relaxation ability. (See "Teaching Imagination Skills to Lower SES Delinquent Youth," *Dissertation Abstracts International,* Section B: The Sciences and Engineering, 58 [6-B], December 1997, 3344 [Ann Arbor, Mich.: University Microfilms International].) My point in mentioning this study is that most youth and adults, even those without early childhood factors that tend to promote and enrich the imaginative capacity, can acquire a greater capacity for creative thinking under the right environmental conditions.

6. John Bell, "Sing a New Song," *Christian Century,* 25 July 2006, p. 22.

nation can flourish — at least to the extent that nature interacting with nurture can allow. For adults, those of us caught or stuck in a work routine, with pressures of bills to pay and calendars that are chock-full of required meetings and deadlines, need to expend some creative effort to find rich fare to feed and nourish our imaginative faculties.

Reading Poems and Fiction in the Local Community

Impediments to an imagination-enriched life include exhaustion — with no energy or attention left over to deal with novelty — distraction, laziness or inertia, and not knowing where to turn or what to do along new, creative lines.[7] That last obstacle is probably the easiest to correct. Here are a few ideas.

Reading poetry — especially reading it aloud with another person — is one of the prime ways we have to exercise our imaginative faculty and open up space for a possible meeting with the Divine. As I have commented already, I suppose most of us don't read poetry because it scares us off as an esoteric practice. We might fear that dipping into a book of poetry would require the mastering of an exotic skill, taking precious time, and thus energy, to engage deeply with poetic symbols and metaphors. In the previous chapter we visited Molly Peacock's work. She tries to reduce the fears that inhibit our poetry reading, and she attempts to facilitate our enjoyment of poetic writing by giving tips on starting a poetry circle. You may be able to get together a group of friends and meet in each other's homes. If that isn't possible, you can always post a sign-up sheet at the local gym or PTA. Bookstores are also frequently willing to provide space and suggestions for both poetry and prose discussion groups.[8]

When selecting a poet's work on which to focus the discussion, browse through bookstores, page through texts, and see what grabs you. Anthologies of poems provide an overview of poets' works by various genres. The poems that spark your interest can then lead you to graze through a (usually) slim volume of the poet's creations, seeing if you find the potential for revelation there.

---

7. Mihaly Csikszentmihalyi, *Creativity: Flow and the Psychology of Discovery and Invention* (New York: HarperCollins Perennial, 1997), p. 344.

8. Molly Peacock, *How to Read a Poem . . . and Start a Poetry Circle* (Toronto: McClelland & Stewart, 1999).

Ideas for which novels to read come from a variety of sources — newspaper reviews, suggestions from friends, the Book Sense Picks list (distributed in independent bookstores and available online), or a general sense of what's au courant. And reading groups for teens are becoming increasingly popular. Whether the group meets to chew over and savor some poems or to digest and discuss one of Shakespeare's plays or the latest novel, at the heart of the discussion circle are what Peacock calls "people who recognize that being deeply affected by language becomes a means to the deeply lived life."[9]

Again, I don't intend to give an exhaustive treatment of practices available in the community that can enrich the imaginative faculty. But let me just say in passing that seeing films — whether at the theater or at home via DVDs or the Internet — can be valuable. In Chapter Three of this book I talked at length about our imagination's enrichment through film. Chosen with spiritual discernment, films can be provocative and open up deep levels of human meaning. Going to the movies is certainly one of the most popular and most accessible ways to exercise our power of imagination and even potentially provide openings for Transcendence.

Other types of creative expression are also available at the community level. If you happen to live in a college or university town, you will likely find plenty of opportunities for creative engagement with the arts. I recently watched excerpts from an hour-long interpretive dance solo that had premiered at Harvard University in May 2004. The dance, with musical accompaniment, included spoken quotations from Descartes's *Discourse on Method* and Kant's "What Is Enlightenment?"[10]

At the end of his work entitled *Creativity,* Mihaly Csikszentmihalyi lists ways to enhance personal creativity, practices gleaned from his work with very imaginative contributors to the culture. He suggests how to spark your curiosity, how to develop habits that will strengthen creative potential (e.g., erect barriers against distraction), and how to choose a special domain to cultivate something new in your life. He comments,

> Much of what makes life interesting and meaningful belongs to special domains: Music, cooking, poetry, gardening, . . . history [and] re-

9. Peacock, *How to Read a Poem,* pp. 209-10.

10. Kimerer Lamothe, "On Fire," presented at the AAR meeting in Washington, D.C., 18 November 2006.

ligion . . . are symbol systems with their own special rules, and they exist outside any individual's life. They and thousands of other such systems make up culture, and we become human by seeing the world through the lenses they provide.[11]

He also points out that delving into these new cultural areas requires effort, and our pet list of "not for me" practices can act as a barrier to imaginative enrichment. Certainly there are creative arenas that just don't agree with us (for me, it's sports; for someone else, it might be dance or philosophy). But more often than not, we fear to tread where we haven't gone before. Consequently, cultural resources in the community remain underutilized. "Either because of ignorance, low self-esteem, or habits of thought established early, we discount the possibility that we could enjoy and be good at many of the things that make others happy."[12]

But such resources exist, both in the community at large (e.g., adult education courses in sculpture such as the one described by Maria Harris,[13] and workshops in icon painting and creative writing), and in educational, artistic, and liturgical practices offered in churches and synagogues. And it is to this latter context for imaginative, enriching practice that we turn next.

Imaginative Practices within Houses of Worship

Those who grew up in homes where religious belief was a way of life remember going to church or synagogue services and having a sense of participating in something that they did not yet understand, but that their grandparents and parents took seriously and that therefore became imprinted in their own memories. Irrespective of anything they might have learned from lessons taught, what likely impressed itself on their minds was the aesthetic character of the experience: the stained-glass windows, the smell of incense, the statues and crosses, the tabernacle where the scroll was kept, the music and procession of clergy and servers as they moved down the center aisle.

My own childhood memories of church are a kaleidoscope of such

11. Csikszentmihalyi, *Creativity*, p. 370.
12. Csikszentmihalyi, *Creativity*, p. 370.
13. Maria Harris, *Teaching and Religious Imagination* (New York: HarperCollins, 1987).

images. I can close my eyes and see in my heart's memory the candles lit at the Christmas Eve service, everyone clutching their own little flickering candles while softly singing "Silent Night" at the end of the service. On Sundays I always sat with my mom and dad in the last pew on the right-hand side of the church. I can see in my imagination's eye the backs of my friends' heads, here and there in the congregation, where they sat with their own families. I absorbed a sense of belonging to a world, to a community of neighbors, in this small town where I grew up, where church and community were bound up with one another. I breathed in the faith of my ancestors, and, like the smell of incense, it has become part of my being's fiber.

A religious way of life is always, of course, a communal affair reflecting a shared, basic understanding about the nature of reality having to do with Transcendence. Typically this understanding of reality affects individual identity first by a process of modeling, and then by practices of initiation, imitation, and instruction. "Religious faith as a way of life is borne . . . by language," Craig Dykstra says, "and each distinct way of life necessarily has a language of its own."[14] Even the names we give our children take on traditional significance. Jews and Christians frequently give their children biblical names in order to remind the children and themselves who they are and to what tradition they belong. My own two sons are named after Celtic and Italian saints, with one of them having the archangel Michael thrown in for good measure!

Thus, religious language, with its own symbols and metaphors and stories, along with ritual and liturgical practices, ensures continuity of meaning over generations, while providing the means to socialize new members into a whole way of life. Dykstra explains, "Certain realities are actually hidden from one who does not live a particular way. . . . With the help of the language that is peculiar to [the communal tradition], there takes place 'a re-shaping of consciousness in which we are given new eyes and new ears.'"[15] And it is the imagination that lies at the heart of this process.

14. Craig Dykstra, "Youth and the Language of Faith," *Religious Education* 81 (1986): 168.

15. Dykstra, "Youth and the Language of Faith," p. 172.

Children and Godly Play

The prime example of a church-based instructional practice that both uses and enriches the child's imagination is Jerome Berryman's method called "Godly play." If religious language is the language of poetry and story with aesthetic, imaginative expression at its core, then this method of instruction embodies all that we've talked about here in these pages. Berryman sees what he terms "theological cognition" as differing from other domains of knowledge, requiring a special way of teaching within the communal setting.[16]

Specifically, children come into the learning space and are welcomed by the class leaders, then gather in a circle symbolizing the faith community. A leader tells a story or a parable or explores a Bible passage, then asks the children to wonder about its meaning, to ask questions. The leader models the process of puzzling over and digesting a story or a reading without prematurely providing answers for closure.

Typically, the children are then asked to choose some visual-art material and go off on their own to express their wondering in their own imaginative way. They have heard a sacred story and then are asked to respond creatively to it within an environment filled with symbols of their faith. Thus, the context supports the connection between language, creative knowing, and the experience of Transcendence. After making their individual creative responses, the children come back together to share their wondering with one another. This time together ends with a shared "meal," modeled on the Eucharistic ritual. In fact, the whole experience takes on, analogously, the form of communal, Eucharistic worship: first hearing the Word in community, then creatively responding to the Word, and finally sharing Eucharistic-like, sacramental nourishment.[17]

The leader's response to the spoken lesson of Godly play not only models a creative openness and wonder, but also is aimed at evoking awareness of even life-and-death issues in the children. For some questions, there are perhaps no firm answers. According to Berryman and others, the children's response to the spoken lesson often reveals

16. Jerome W. Berryman, *Godly Play* (San Francisco: HarperSanFrancisco, 1991). See also his more recent work, *The Complete Guide to Godly Play*, 3 vols. (Denver, Colo.: Living the Good News, 2002).

17. Berryman, *Godly Play*, pp. 24-41.

their own concerns with issues of limits, unknowable mystery, and finally death.[18]

The unspoken lesson, the implicit meaning inherent in the whole learning process, ideally gives the children a safe haven or sanctuary where they can be open to explore, to risk confrontation with life-and-death issues. The open door where they are welcomed represents hospitality to all who cross the threshold; and the openness of wondering creates an experience of Transcendence, the spiritual sense of the divine, mysterious Presence coming to meet them in the wonder and worship.[19] Although this method of instruction was developed within a Christian framework, the basic principles of responding to a sacred text with questioning wonder, within a safe communal setting, could be adapted by other faith traditions.

Obviously, worship communities differ widely in the programs they offer children and youth. In the parish where I was pastor, we used a variation of Berryman's method. To do so effectively requires staff leaders, physical space, and a variety of resources that most churches could put together with some dedication and effort. But if you're searching for a spiritual learning environment for your child, there are some basic elements that you would probably look for — and Karen-Marie Yust enumerates some of these in her book titled *Real Kids, Real Faith*.

For example, you would look carefully at whether the congregation welcomes children's participation in liturgy. Are children's spiritual lives nurtured? Are their parents' spirits nurtured? Are there visible symbols of the tradition displayed? Are both contemporary and traditional hymns sung? Are preaching and teaching examples drawn from traditional sacred texts as well as from contemporary life? These are only some of the questions Yust raises in her book, but all are important in evaluating the practices that feed and nourish the imagination of the young as well as the imagination of their parents.[20]

---

18. Berryman, *Godly Play*, pp. 62-63.
19. Berryman, *Godly Play*, pp. 79-109.
20. Karen-Marie Yust, *Real Kids, Real Faith* (San Francisco: Jossey-Bass, 2004).

Ritual and Liturgical Practices

Mary Karr, author of the best seller *The Liars' Club,* recently wrote a book called *Sinners Welcome* in which she explores part of her life odyssey, which took her through the doors of a Roman Catholic Church and finally into the embrace of a life-changing faith. She describes an early experience in the church this way:

> Through the simple physical motions I followed during Mass (me, *following* something?), our bodies standing and sitting and kneeling in concert, I often felt my mind grow quiet, and my surface differences from others began to be obliterated. . . . So the exercises during Mass . . . made me feel like part of a tribe, in a way, and the effect carried over in me even after church.[21]

It was first in the practice of ritual, in the performance of embodied symbols of faith, that she opened herself to the possibilities of worship within a faith community.

Doing ritual is a powerful way of "saying" your meaning within a communal framework. (Even if done at home, the ritual takes on communal meaning as the practitioner engages in bodily language rooted in traditional religious significance.) But as we just saw in Berryman's Godly play, performing ritual also has cognitive and emotional effects that shape the practitioner's consciousness and sense of reality (as reflected in Karr's reported experience). I've already reviewed the essence of ritual actions in this chapter. Suffice it to say here that liturgy — the written, story-shaped meaning expressed in language — is fleshed out and completed by ritual action, as the latter is shaped and informed by the tradition's sacred stories.

The center of Christian liturgical rituals is the Eucharistic set of ritual acts commemorating and sacramentally re-experiencing Jesus' Last Supper. We took an in-depth look at that ritual in Chapter One. But there are also many rituals within religious traditions that mark milestones in an individual's life: baptism or briss, confirmation or bar mitzvah, marriage, reconciliation, anointing, and healing are all rituals that become in a sense rites of passage from one condition to another. Again, these embodied expressions and the narrative roots that give

21. Mary Karr, *Sinners Welcome* (New York: HarperCollins, 2006).

them meaning all spring from the human imagination. According to Herbert Anderson and Edward Foley, these rituals "shape our stories, and our instinct to perceive life as a narrative urges us to rehearse that narrative through our bodies."[22]

Death Rituals

As an example of a milestone ritual as imaginative practice, Anderson and Foley describe ritual practices around the experience of dying and death. Not all of these rituals take place within houses of worship, but in our society, when someone dies — even if the family rarely darkened the door of a church — the kin typically seek out a pastor or a rabbi to say the words and do the thing that matters.

Before the death, the one who is dying might write an autobiography, or create a videotape for children or grandchildren, telling his or her story and in so doing imaginatively create a sense of wholeness to his or her life. After the death, the living who mourn can write a biography of their loved one, and in the telling they can both create and express their own sense of meaning of their loved one's life. "If a dying individual's review of life is honest, complete, and accessible," say Anderson and Foley, "it is . . . easier to construct an authentic memory that facilitates mourning."[23]

Before the death, one ritual action that can fill the participants' imaginations with comforting images of healing and wholeness is anointing, accompanied by prayers of thanksgiving for the loved one's life. With perhaps all of the family joining in, such a ritual creates and expresses a sense of communal ties with the one who is dying. Sometimes this gathering also provides a time for honest reflection on the lives shared, and an opportunity for expressions of love, reconciliation, and forgiveness for past hurts.[24]

---

22. Herbert Anderson and Edward Foley, *Mighty Stories, Dangerous Rituals* (San Francisco: Jossey-Bass, 1998), p. 27.

23. Anderson and Foley, *Mighty Stories, Dangerous Rituals,* p. 99.

24. Anderson and Foley also describe what they refer to as a "litany of 'lasts.'" Once everyone, including the one who is dying, acknowledges the irreversibility of the dying process that is under way, all can begin to make something special of the last time events happen — the last Christmas, the last anniversary, the last luncheon out, the last time a visit takes place, and so on. While this might seem like a somewhat morbid ritual to carry

Rituals surrounding wakes and viewings of the body differ markedly by culture and geography.[25] In general, funerals and interments in our culture — embodied expressions of thanksgiving and stark separation — are for the sake of the living. And the rituals embedded in these liturgical practices are shaped by the community's views of death and what follows. For traditions that embrace in their collective imagination a sense of afterlife with God, ritual practices and prayers include an intercession for God's mercy for the dead and comfort for the still living.

Finally, during the period of acute mourning, stories of the dead loved one are important to retell and share, to give comfort and to hold in memory those who are still dear. Along these lines, the creative celebration of anniversaries and birthdays by the ritual lighting of candles and the saying of prayers is a continuing way to celebrate a life that remains significant even in death.

The Development of New Rituals

New rituals develop to meet our human needs for creation and expression of meaning in our lives. I talked about my own lighting of an oil lamp at the breakfast table as a personally meaningful creation of sacred space and time before morning prayers. But some events occur that are unanticipated eruptions or significant transitions in the life cycle and that require a communal context for imaginative expression.

Events such as divorce, retirement, and the withdrawal of life support for a loved one provide occasions that call for ritual observance. Anderson and Foley list rules for the creation of new rituals. Among other things, they warn against making the ritual itself too complicated. "A single act of blessing, laying of flowers, burning of a document, or handing over a gift (for example, a ring) may be far more effective than piling a number of ritual gestures together."[26]

---

out, it can also be an opening for honest speaking from the heart and an "invitation to mourn."

25. The first time I attended a Southern Baptist wake, I was struck by the dramatic displays of grief before the family member's open casket.

26. Anderson and Foley, *Mighty Stories, Dangerous Rituals*, p. 130.

Music, Art, and Dance: Adult Godly Play

Folks like Mary Karr who wander into a church looking for something that they never before embraced ("seekers," in current parlance), as well as adults who were raised in religious homes and have now struck out on their own to fashion their own faith journey, go through a process known as catechesis, or instruction in the traditions of a new religious way of life. Like the children who participate in Godly play, such seekers learn the faith by exposure to traditional symbols, by hearing and responding to stories, and by the practice of liturgy within a safe community providing hospitality to all who come. Thus, these adults come to learn the faith tradition through imaginative practice.

Trends have appeared in the last decade designed to attract seekers to the Christian tradition and provide church-based teaching and practices to acquaint them with a religious way of life. The Alpha video series, created in England by the evangelical wing of the Anglican communion, is an example of such an effort. Another example in this country is the Emergent Church movement, which combines traditional symbols, creeds, sermons, and ritual practices with art displays. Communal worship practices usually include the offering of music, which is nontraditional (although the lyrics may be quite orthodox), loud, and participatory, and which has been likened to the sound of contemporary grunge!

There *is* something elemental about music, a topic I touched on in Chapter One. As Jeremy Begbie points out, the making of music arises out of the rhythms of our bodies themselves. The beat of our hearts, the stamp of our feet, the clap of our hands — all of these reflect the source of music and song in the body.[27] Others have pointed out that people are brought together in the joy of making music, and singing together is a reflection of our creative freedom as human beings. Hearts as well as minds become open to new meaning through song.

The language of the imagination expressed in music and other art forms is subtle and at times even ephemeral, with thoughts and desires expressed through movement, song, and other symbolic forms without

27. Jeremy Begbie, *Theology, Music, and Time* (New York: Cambridge University Press, 2000), pp. 15, 26-28.

28. Dykstra, "Youth and the Language of Faith," p. 181.

a sense of closure. Craig Dykstra suggests that perhaps this is one reason why singing in the church choir is for many of our youth the most "profoundly affecting introduction to religious language."[28] Although some teens might be reluctant to speak about God or religious longings to one another, singing such imaginings can be emotionally powerful. And music — including apparently even of the grunge variety — moves all of us and affects us deeply in ways beyond what words can tell.

Tim Keel, pastor of an emergent church called Jacob's Well in Kansas City, Missouri, is a cofounder of the Emergent Church movement. He says, "If most evangelicals follow a pattern of believe-behave-belong, we reverse that pattern and make it belong-behave-believe. We say, 'Try on these clothes, take up these practices, and see what happens.'"[29] Actually, the idea that cognitive changes occur as a result of behavioral practices rests on pretty solid psychological ground. Within ancient religious tradition there is also embedded the notion that praying shapes believing. My assumption here, of course, is that the imagination both shapes and is shaped by ritual, and thus mediates between embodied symbol and conscious expression. (In any case, Jacob's Well is now attracting a thousand attenders every week, so they must be doing something right!)

If the imagination's expression in all forms of art provides a link between the Divine and the human, between the Transcendent and the mundane, then it would seem that the church and synagogue would be fitting places to engage with various art forms. Visual art displayed in stained-glass windows and seen in sculptured figures, musical art performed by organists and choirs — these have always been a part of religious worship experience. And although art used for liturgical purposes should primarily function in the service of worship, it should also be aesthetically pleasing to the ear and eye.

The relationship between artists and organized religion has not always been a very easy one. Suspicion has lurked on both sides. Artists have been wary of being used as propagandists for churches' evangelistic causes, fearing an attempt to control their creative expression. Churches in turn have historically resisted works of art as idols to be worshiped or as purveyors of secular humanism and blasphemous subject matter. And historically, I suppose, most of us who inhabit the Western, post-Enlightenment world have tended to favor the cognitive, the

29. Jason Byassee, "Emerging Model," *Christian Century,* 19 September 2006, p. 23.

written word over the visual form. But if art forms created out of an inspired imagination provide a link between humans and transcendent Mystery — by getting "hold of the invisible, penetrat[ing] as far as possible into the visible"[30] — then houses of worship are an ideal place to engage with art in its many forms.

One of the best practical guides I have run across in this area is Fiona Bond's *The Arts in Your Church*. Bond begins by providing a nuts-and-bolts discussion of how to hold art shows in the church. She discusses what needs to be done before the show — planning, raising money, securing the artist(s), marketing, and understanding the law — and what needs to be done afterwards: reviewing aspects of failure and success to inform future planning. Next Bond gives a series of case studies that are both concrete and illuminating.[31] I'll highlight three of them here.

The first case study was conducted by Jeremy Begbie, who directs the "Theology Through the Arts" program at both Cambridge and the University of St. Andrews in Scotland.[32] In meeting with a group of singers and musicians, Begbie decided to carry out a Bible study with them. After reading Matthew's scene describing the baptism of Jesus by John the Baptist, he asked the artists to "hear" the passage musically and interpret it with sound.

Begbie concludes that the experience was a genuine Bible study, entering the world of Scripture through music. "The players were glued to the text with the intensity of a biblical scholar." He emphasizes that the music, with power of its own, helped penetrate the biblical text in a fresh way.[33] In this case the players were using their own musical talent — which was natural to them — to interpret the text. The singers did the same. But the sacred text could also be interpreted using almost any type of art form — poetry, dance, sculpture and other visual art.

In the spirit of this most practical resource, Begbie lists concrete points to be kept in mind when planning and leading such an imaginative practice. For example, allow plenty of time for the experience; join

---

30. Brian Hearne, "God's Story in Our Story," *African Ecclesial Review* 26 (1984): 43.

31. Fiona Bond, *The Arts in Your Church* (Carlisle, U.K.: Piquant Press, 2001). Bond's book is intended primarily for the British market, so what she writes about legal matters isn't necessarily applicable in the United States.

32. Jeremy Begbie, "Sounds of Scripture," in Bond, *The Arts in Your Church,* pp. 55-58.

33. Begbie, "Sounds of Scripture," p. 56.

in as leader; avoid telling the participants what to play — or draw or sculpt; allow periods of silence for intuition (God's Spirit?) to do its work; and assure the participants that "mistakes" are O.K. so that they'll be willing to take risks and explore.[34]

Two other fascinating case studies reported by Bond involve the visual arts. Andrew Bonner writes about the Cornerstone Arts Festival, originating out of an evangelical Anglican church in the west end of Glasgow. It reportedly grew from a modest idea involving a drama group producing a small revue to a three-day arts festival that was part of a city-wide celebration of Glasgow as the U.K.'s Capital of Architecture and Design in 1999. In the end, it included an impressive range of offerings:

> . . . a comedy-revue plus a new play, a dance drama, a children's musical event, a visual art installation along with an art exhibition, bands and musicians, percussion workshops, poetry recitals, storytelling, and a special Sunday night service in which five members of the congregation would share the stories of how one significant work of art had shaped their personal growth in faith.

Bonner also presents a detailed description of the planning process and concludes by providing lessons the group learned. For example, asking for donations instead of admission charges worked well, but their marketing had been somewhat inadequate, and they didn't fully capitalize on opportunities to reach beyond their own congregation.[35]

The other case study involving visual art is presented by Julia Price and her colleagues. This idea started as a kitchen-table conversation among contemporary art lovers and grew into a project, supported by a grant from London's Millennium Commission, funding art displays in sacred spaces, creating an "art trail" through twelve churches in towns near London.[36] Some of the artists who were secured were controversial because of the content of their visual creations, and thus the event got wide media play.

---

34. Begbie, "Sounds of Scripture," p. 58.

35. Andrew Bonner, "Cornerstone Arts Festival," in Bond, *The Arts in Your Church*, pp. 59-63.

36. Since much of modern art — using physical installations, performance pieces, video art, and so on — invites the viewer to collaborate in a creative process of interpretation, the process of engagement becomes one of co-creation with the artist.

The authors admit there were some inherent limits presented by the church settings: lighting was less than ideal for art display, security was limited, furnishings and wall colors were fixed, and some church venues had less-than-desirable wall space for displays. But they note how amazing it was that the event happened in the first place. Secular artists, several of whom never set foot in churches, were willing to work with houses of worship that, in turn, opened their doors to partner with some whose art was viewed as shocking. (It should be noted here that the most controversial artist shifted her subject matter to collaborate with local children in producing a quilt titled "Show Me Something Beautiful.") This event turned out to be an astonishing success, opening doors for future collaborations and thus breaking down some of the age-old barriers that have existed between churches and artistic communities.[37]

At the very least, such projects provide an opening for dialogue between various faith communities and local artists. I believe some limits do need to be set on suitability for display in sacred spaces. After all, not all imaginative products express meetings with transcendent Mystery, and some have the potential for expressing and creating evil effects in those who engage them.

Thus, there needs to be some discerning assessment of the potential for human flourishing as an outcome of engagement with artistic pieces. Nevertheless, the case studies in Bond's book — ranging from visual art to music and dance to the art of storytelling — are concrete and fruitful examples of ways to exercise the imaginative capacity and to meet the Divine through artistic expression.

Stories in the Church

Churches and synagogues are places that house and nurture our sacred stories — our personal life stories and faith journeys that we share with one another, as well as our founding story of hope and salvation that gives final meaning to our lives. Here we'll consider the practices of both storytelling and story interpretation, which shape and enrich our imaginations as places to meet God.

---

37. Julia Porter Price, Ann Mullins, and Paul Lowe, "Engaging with Contemporary Culture through Contemporary Art," in Bond, *The Arts in Your Church,* pp. 76-80.

Houses of Worship as Places for Our Stories

We make meaning by conversation; we create meaning in our lives through the give-and-take of shared stories. Mary Karr (whom I quoted earlier), began to pray after a conversation with a poet friend she admired who casually mentioned his prayer practice. She was shocked that he actually did such a thing, and she began talking to him about how he did it, what he said, and why. And so she thought she'd give it a try, she who'd been agnostic at best all her life. Karr was at first surprised and then awed by the experience, and over time she felt joy and peace in the process. She, in turn, has shared her story in essay form, and I expect this tale of her own faith journey has opened the imagination of untold numbers of readers to the possibility of God.[38]

The Church of the Holy Apostles is a large Episcopal church in the Chelsea neighborhood of New York City. During the early 1990s, the writer Ian Frazier received a grant to develop a writer's workshop at an urban outreach place of his choice. He choose the Church of the Holy Apostles, which runs a very active soup kitchen for the needy in that area. With the help of two other writers, Frazier has run this weekly workshop since then, with a dozen or so homeless persons participating during any given meeting.

Frazier says, "It's satisfying . . . to write a self-revealing cry or shout and lay it out for people to see, and to find patterns and beauty even in pain. . . . It's one of the noble acts humans do, and almost always it ennobles those who do it." The workshop is based on the premise that telling one's story is healing and makes for a sense of wholeness in one's life. The participants meet weekly over the lunch hour and are given a topic on which they may (or may not) write. Focusing on such topics as "my first love," "the worst night," "my mother," "the most humiliating thing that ever happened to me," "my wish list," "religion," and "a new door opens," they draft stories and then share them with each other for response and sometimes critique. The best of these stories have been published in a book titled *Food for the Soul*.[39]

Many of these stories are moving and at times heart-wrenching.

---

38. Karr, "Facing Altars: Poetry and Prayer," *Sinners Welcome,* pp. 69-93.

39. Elizabeth Maxwell and Susan Shapiro, eds., *Food for the Soul* (New York: Church Publishing Company, 2004).

But this workshop has provided a welcome opportunity for its partici-pants to tell the stories of their lives in a safe place, to create — perhaps for the first time — a meaningful whole, experiencing spiritual healing in the process. As the editors note in the introduction to the book, pub-lishing these stories has given voice to those who usually remain voice-less. It has also clearly shown that such narrative creativity is a mark of being human, irrespective of one's situation in life.

Margaret Silf describes what she calls a "head and feet approach" to enhance and fulfill our spiritual journeys. Following the ancient practice of having a "soul friend," she suggests you form a partnership with another — a wise friend or a spiritual advisor who becomes a part-ner in your spiritual journey. Soul friends listen to each other's stories, the spiritual insights and longings beneath the mundane aspects of our lives: "What is my deepest desire?" "What do I cling to for my security?" "Where was God or my sense of Other when my father died?" They also intuit God's mystery working beneath the surface of the everyday, and they address gently and lovingly but prophetically what each sees in the process. "A person without a soul friend," Silf says, "is like a body with-out a head."[40] Thus, soul friends — frequently found in or attached to religious communities (I found my own soul friend, a Roman Catholic priest, through a mutual church friend) — accompany you on your life's journey.[41]

And so it is in conversation with one another that we can be touched by grace and we can imaginatively see God's work in the story of our lives. Churches and synagogues can be — should be — safe places for sharing stories of each other's faith journey and helping each other see God's "footprints" in our lives.

40. Margaret Silf, *Companions of Christ: Ignatian Spirituality for Everyday Living* (Grand Rapids: William B. Eerdmans, 2005), p. 90.

41. Within the Ignatian spiritual tradition, the soul friend or spiritual advisor works with you in meditating on the *Spiritual Exercises* we discussed earlier, sometimes in a thirty-day retreat at a local retreat center or monastery, sometimes in sessions spread out over a nine-month period. In following the exercises as a meditative practice, one con-fronts the deepest questions of one's life (for example: What is the shape of my life's story so far? Where is God in it? What is my life about now and where is it going?).

Houses of Worship as Places for Savoring God's Word

The story of salvation across the pages of Scripture is that story we learn to interpret within the Judeo-Christian faith tradition. Other traditions have other founding stories, but this has been our focus here. And for Christians, it's that story which in turn interprets our lives. But in general, I believe that places of worship should be houses where people can read and wonder together, can ask questions and puzzle over the meaning of stories drawn from their own ancient traditions. And like any other aesthetic practice, the art of interpretation — engaging our imaginations, which create meaning for our lives and hope for our futures — needs to be taught.

Churches educate youth and adults in the language of theology and Scripture, introducing them to the sacred texts and making those writings imaginatively come to life through conversations about the meaning of metaphors, images, stories, parables, symbols, and concepts. As Craig Dykstra and others have pointed out, the language used within the church community has to be clear, but rich enough to have some real bearing on actual Monday-morning reality, and not just Sunday-morning lives. It also has to be dynamic and open enough to allow questions, along with vital interpretation and contemporary application.

"When things are heard, if words do not reach the ears of the heart, nothing happens." So says a Sufi mystic — and there is truth in his words. Simply translating the Scripture stories and poems into morals and doctrines and rules to be followed, without touching the emotions and the heart — the whole person — is inadequate and hardly exercises or enriches the imagination. In the best of situations, teachers within churches and synagogues guide youth and adult seekers in what can be viewed as "aesthetic encounters" with the narratives and parables found in Scripture. An arresting element in the story — a twist, a surprise, a contradiction, a puzzle — if taken in, savored, and felt, can have a stunning effect on the reader or hearer, stimulating life-and-death questions and basic wondering related to the learner's own life. Again, such imaginative engagement, along faithful lines, needs both the tradition of the community to guide interpretation as well as the seeker's enriched, imaginative application in his or her own life within a community shared with others.

Reading and interpreting, imaginatively grappling with the meaning of Bible stories, are part of the process to enliven Scripture for our everyday lives. But to be able to know the story in such a way that you can actually tell it faithfully is to weave the story into the very fabric of your life — into your flesh and into your heart. An organization I discovered when preparing to write this chapter provides resources that can help you do this.

The Network of Biblical Storytellers (NOBS; www.nobs.org) provides books, audiocassettes, CDs, videotapes, and DVDs to assist in biblical storytelling. Encouraging a variety of imaginative expressions of traditional sacred stories, including oral, written, and electronic modes, NOBS advocates "all kinds of storytelling but commends especially the practice of telling the texts as they've been traditioned to us." The organizers envision biblical storytelling as a spiritual discipline involving what they call committing the story to "deep memory" — internalizing the story as image and feeling, making the story become part of you in the process. Then you will be equipped to engage the text in a lively telling, "a sacred act that binds teller and listeners in community." I view this kind of resource as potentially very helpful, particularly if it is used within a church or synagogue workshop setting, with interpretive guidance as part of the shaping process.[42]

Father Gregory Fruehwirth, an Episcopal priest and monk who's a friend of mine, talked recently about our imaginative life that we populate with saints such as St. Francis of Assisi and Julian of Norwich. "At the level of the intuition and imagination," Father Gregory says, "the Saints actually live, and their presence is directly known, with all their wild stories and eccentric temperaments and beautiful devotion." The same can be said for the biblical characters who come alive in our imaginations — Job and Jonah, John the Baptist, Mary and Jesus, and the rest. They populate our imaginations "as outposts of heaven," inspiring our daily lives and our discernment of what enriches us and what destroys us. And God does in fact work through these figures who are alive for us now in our mind's images. God inspires us through our en-

42. For example, The Telling Place offers training courses in biblical storytelling at their headquarters in Northumbria, England. This organization also gives one-day workshops in the art of storytelling around that country. In addition, it maintains links with the Network of Biblical Storytellers in the United States. The Web site posts regional events and gatherings, and in addition to books and a journal, has a registry of biblical storytellers and provides a useful bibliography.

riched imaginative capacity, stimulating our passions. As my friend says, "Knowing them, we glimpse what we are to become."[43]

PREACHING THE WORD AS AN IMAGINATIVE PRACTICE   The practice of giving and receiving sermons is an exercise in imaginative engagement. In recent years, a focus on what's come to be called the "new homiletic" emphasizes the use of rhetorical skills in the service of persuasion. Preachers are coached in a narrative style of delivery, telling the sacred stories in a way that evokes the emotions of the hearers and opens them up imaginatively to a new vision of life. The congregation comes to hear their own life stories told and reshaped in the process. With less emphasis on rational argument and more emphasis on metaphorical, aesthetic language that feeds the imaginative powers of the listeners, the weekly affirmation of a religious worldview that expresses faith without limits and finality is experienced by those who hear the preached Word of God in narrative form.

Thus, the role that imagination and creative expression play in the proclamation of faith is founded not on rational certainties but on the openness of wonder and questioning of mystery experienced in the lives of those present. The power of language to move the seeker, opening up a grace-filled shaft of light between heaven and earth, is thus founded on the creative potency of the imagination, and fosters a co-creation of meaning in the dialogue opened up between the preacher and the one who hungers to hear that life and the world have meaning after all.

WALKING THE WALK WITH IMAGINATIVE PRACTICES   The stories of our faith may provide imaginative glimpses of what we are to become, but it is only in actually living out the meaning of these stories in our daily lives that we are transformed. While our faith journey begins by having someone to talk with — a parent, a neighbor, a mentor, a soul friend — it is actualized in the daily practices flowing from the world of meaning that our imaginations create out of such dialogue.

Karen-Marie Yust suggests a number of ways that children can exercise their faith imaginatively, including collecting for UNICEF at Hallow-

---

43. Chapter talk from Julian House of the Order of Julian of Norwich (Waukesha, Wisconsin), written by Father Gregory, 31 October 2006.

een and creating "care bags" for children with long-term illnesses, whether in hospitals or at home (e.g., filling bags with puzzle books, coloring books and crayons, tablets and colored pencils, and so on).[44] We can encourage them to think of others in addition to themselves at holidays. In the church where I was pastor for a number of years, the young people made gifts to take to our elderly shut-ins at Christmastime, and they participated as "hosts" for Caritas, our annual turn to provide overnight shelter and food for the homeless in Richmond. This yearly activity, as well as monthly preparation and serving of meals in a park that was a gathering place for the homeless, put "flesh" on the bones of biblical stories of hospitality, and imaginatively enriched their lives in the process.

Various contributors to Fiona Bond's book (discussed earlier) describe cases of successful community outreach from churches using the arts as a means of imaginative engagement. Contributor Andrew Rumsey describes Romsey Mill, a youth and community center in Cambridge, England, which was set up by local churches in 1980 to serve the needs of young families and youth who faced social marginalization. Such reaching out has to be done with care, Rumsey notes: "As churches become increasingly sealed off from the communities in which they are set, outreach can easily become Star Trek–style excursions from the mother ship into alien territory, with all the awkwardness and bad acting that involves." Communicating effectively in this case involved using music, drama, and games to introduce young people to issues of faith and to draw them out. "Communication meant listening as well as speaking," Rumsey explains, "enabling the stranger's voice to be heard so that who they were could intersect in authentic ways with who God is." And their engagement with various forms of art was central to the process, eliciting discussion and fostering new images for those at-risk youth of what they could become.[45]

*   *   *

We began this book with William James's observation that the mark of genuine religious experience, the evidence that you and I have opened

---

44. Yust, *Real Kids, Real Faith,* pp. 154-55.

45. Andrew Rumsey, "Meeting the Neighbours: Community Arts and Youth Mission at Romsey Mill," in Bond, *The Arts in Your Church,* pp. 81-82.

our imagination to Transcendence and have indeed been met by God, is reflected in the good fruits of our lives, leading to our own flourishing as well as that of our family and our community.

Lately I've been struck by the realization that no matter what I've accomplished in life, I possess nothing — not my intelligence, not my imaginative skills, not my health, not my cultural advantages — I possess nothing that I have not been given. And I can never pay back all these riches — not to my parents, my country, or God. But you and I do have resources to "pay it forward." Margaret Silf suggests that every time a good thing happens to us, we should do something good for three others, walking the walk of faith, putting into actions the fruits of our imagination and prayers.[46]

Over these last two chapters, we have considered "Godly play" in all its forms, exercising and enriching the imagination of children and adults through imaginative practices in the home, the community, and houses of worship. Kierkegaard once observed that God uses the imagination to draw us toward reality, leading us far and deep into human existence. And when the imagination has helped us to go as far as we can, that is just where true reality begins. It is my contention here that nothing is more important than that quest for truth.

46. Silf, *Companions of Christ,* p. 107.

CHAPTER SIX

Concluding Thoughts:
The Imagination and the Making of Meaning

Life was charmed but without politics or religion. It was the life of the children of the pioneers — life after God — a life of earthly salvation on the edge of heaven. . . . I think there was a trade-off somewhere along the line. I think the price we paid for our golden life was an inability to fully believe in love; instead we gained an irony that scorched everything it touched. And I wonder if this irony is the price we paid for the loss of God.

Douglas Coupland, *Life after God*[1]

In the religious view of reality, all phenomena point toward that which transcends them, and this transcendence actively impinges from all sides on the empirical sphere of human existence. . . . This [rediscovery of the supernatural] in no way implies remoteness from the moral challenges of the moment, but rather the most careful attention to each human gesture that we encounter or that we may be called upon to perform in the everyday dramas of human life — literally, an "infinite care" in the affairs of men — just because . . . it is in the midst of these affairs that "some have entertained angels unawares" (Hebrews 13:2).

Peter Berger, *A Rumor of Angels*[2]

1. Douglas Coupland, *Life after God* (New York: Simon & Schuster/Pocket Books, 1994), p. 273.

2. Peter Berger, *A Rumor of Angels* (Garden City, N.Y.: Doubleday/Anchor Books, 1969), pp. 94-95.

The concluding chapter of any work gives an author one last chance to make her point — maybe the *first* chance if you are like me and skim the last chapter of a book before making that initial commitment to come along for the whole ride. If you have traveled with me this far, you will recognize the basic point that I have expressed in various ways in the introduction and the last five chapters. And that point is this: Religious belief is grounded in our experience of Transcendence (however we define that Other) by the power of our imagination to meet God in the world around us. These gleanings of God we meet by intuition are imaginatively expressed through symbol and metaphor and ritual, through song and through story. These glimmers prompt worship in some form and a deep sense that life has meaning beyond our own finite limits.

But I have also argued here that our creative power can give rise to both good and evil imaginings, that it can run amok if not rooted in community wisdom. Thus, I believe that the cultural symbols and stories that feed our imaginations — through which Transcendence can be encountered — must be formed within the context of a living tradition. Specifically, a basic sense that life has some ultimate meaning and the worship that flows from this sense is founded on, and informed by, the wisdom of a religious tradition or culture — here a Judeo-Christian, Western heritage.

In these concluding remarks I want to return to where we began this journey and look again at our contemporary culture, describing in a bit more detail where you and I find ourselves today. In the process, I'll highlight the main path we have traveled together, and shine the clearest light I can on the road ahead.

The American Dream: The Good Life?

Up until now, I have not emphasized our unique American cultural scene because my discussion has been aimed at what I believe is the essential core of being human — that is, our ability to create meaning through the imagination's power to draw elements from experience and symbolically make something new within the human community. Nevertheless, you and I live in a particular place and time, in a culture that shapes us continuously and pervasively, in ways often hidden from our awareness or reflection. Our cultural products, our culture's stories and sacred myths given to our imagination, provide the elements for our creative meaning-making, whether we are fully aware of it or not. So I think it would be useful to pause at this late stage of our travel together and look a bit more closely at that culture.

David Brooks, the *New York Times* columnist, wrote a popular book several years ago entitled *On Paradise Drive*. Although in many ways Brooks engages in hyperbole and caricature in describing the contemporary American scene, in other ways his description of our national character and its setting rings true. Brooks, as well as many other social commentators, basically sees us Americans as materialistic, hedonistic, naive, competitive, restless, striving, and above all, as individualistic in outlook.[3]

Yet the American dream, which colors and motivates our imaginings, is also basically filled with hope for an ideal future of perfection and bliss, of utopia and blessedness blossoming on these shores. This dream of blessedness drives us and draws us perpetually onward to new horizons, new ventures on which to gamble, new battles to win. Brooks puts it this way:

> Born in abundance, inspired by opportunity, nurtured in imagination, spiritualized by a sense of God's blessing and call, and realized in ordinary life day by day, this Paradise Spell is the controlling ideology of American life. Just out of reach, just beyond the next ridge, just with the next home . . . or diet plan; just with the next political hero, the next credit-card purchase, or the next true love; just with the right all-terrain vehicle . . . the right motivational seminar; just with the right schools . . . and the proper morality; just with the right beer . . . the next technology or the next shopping spree, there is this spot you can get to where all tensions will melt, all time pressures are relieved, and all contentment can be realized. Prosperity will be joined with virtue, materialism with idealism, achievement with equality, success with love . . . thereby producing a new Eden.[4]

Brooks sees this "Paradise Spell" at the root of our drive to work seven days a week, to consume as if there were no tomorrow, and to

---

3. David Brooks, *On Paradise Drive* (New York: Simon & Schuster, 2004).
4. Brooks, *On Paradise Drive*, pp. 268-69.

embrace New Age experiences of the wildest variety, longing for redemption from any source that promises it.

Brooks concludes his analysis of the American character this way: "At the start of this book . . . I asked if we are as shallow as we look. No, we are not. We are an imaginative, a dreaming people."[5] By that I suppose he means that we are fundamentally a hope-filled people, perhaps narcissistic and individualistic to the core, but driven by our imaginations to strive for paradise, for wholeness, for some version of God's Kingdom on earth.

Of course I have argued throughout this book that we have a built-in longing for Transcendence, a longing for release from the mundane, a longing to transcend our own finite limits of mortality, a longing to meet God or the transcendent Other beneath and beyond the ordinary of our everyday lives. For many, this longing is ungrounded in a religious tradition or culture. And because of the secular social, educational, legal, and political culture we Americans inhabit, this longing is expressed and given shape by our imaginations within a pluralistic scene, where tolerance has become the cardinal virtue.

Thus, on our own in a pragmatic, materialistic society, we tend to celebrate and embrace the advancement of ourselves and our own goods and ultimately our own happiness. The pursuit of individual happiness is not new to our American vision; indeed, it was an express part of our founding fathers' ideal of inalienable rights. But in former times this pursuit of personal happiness was bounded by moral strictures such as a shared moral order that restrained acts of sexual display and the nature of public speech. Now the pursuit of my own happiness is an end in itself, unbounded by a shared sense of a single moral order and a cultural consensus regarding the common good.

So Brooks argues that what pragmatically works for me, what speaks to me and advances my own happiness, is what I embrace at the moment, at least provisionally. And what works for you advances your happiness, and all is held at least tentatively as good if it works, at least for the time being. "What may be true for you may not be true for me," Brooks says. "What may be true for me now might not be true for me later. Therefore, it is important not to judge others too harshly, because we are all pursuing our own horizons."[6]

5. Brooks, *On Paradise Drive,* p. 281.
6. Brooks, *On Paradise Drive,* p. 277.

It is the premise of this book, of course, that some things are ultimately true and therefore matter very much. Thus, taking such a neutral stance runs counter to the basic assumptions of this book — that God exists, that God or a transcendent Other impinges on our consciousness, and that we create meaning for our lives by being attuned to such transcendent revelation, expressing our intuitive glimpses of God through various creative forms.[7]

So I have pursued this project in reaction against our New Age, individualistic, postmodern Zeitgeist, just as Coleridge and James wrote against the philosophical and scientific rationalism of their day. I have joined my voice with that of Peter Berger, who, in the 1970s, wrote the best-selling book *A Rumor of Angels*. In it he encouraged the secularists and scoffers of religion in his day to follow an inductive method to uncover traces of God "hiding in nooks and crannies of the culture."[8]

Berger saw such "signals of Transcendence" present in the history and traditions of the three great monotheistic religions of Judaism, Christianity, and Islam, as well as in cultural creative expressions such as Gothic cathedrals, the music of Bach and Mozart, the poetry of Hölderlin, and the artworks of Chagall. He saw in people (and Berger was writing to Americans of my generation) a "fundamental religious impulse" to respond to such signals of Transcendence in worship. "It is in worship that the prototypical gesture of religion is realized again and again. This is the gesture in which man reaches out in hope toward transcendence."[9]

Berger wrote his little book within what he viewed as a primarily secular culture, a culture without enchantment, a culture flattened and emptied of religious sentiments and ritual by its pursuit of material goods, saturated by affluence, a culture where only the rumor of angels remained to fill our need for something more. But "if the signals of transcendence have become rumors in our time," he said, "then we can

---

7. Throughout this book I have also taken a more nuanced and positive position regarding the potential benefits of pluralism. Our postmodern, pluralistic culture fosters openness to new possibilities, encourages questioning and wonder, and permits pushing beyond the limits of known boundaries to explore, in dialogue, the Mystery beyond traditional certitudes.

8. Berger, *A Rumor of Angels,* p. 24.

9. Berger, *A Rumor of Angels,* p. 87.

set out to explore these rumors — and perhaps to follow them up to their source."[10]

We are children of our times, and our imaginations are colored and shaped by our social matrix. We cannot escape the technological, secular, scientific world we live in. But nor do I think we want to go back to a pre-Enlightenment world of autocratic authority and superstition. We hear the rumor of angels, and we long for something more beyond the mundane, but we feel the pull of rationalism, the postmodern pull of skepticism. We struggle between the worlds of belief and unbelief, of hope and cynicism.

Charles Taylor eloquently describes this tug between rational science and postmodern skepticism on the one hand and this sense of something more on the other, this haunting rumor of angels that you and I may also feel, being children of our culture. And he says that in order to navigate our world, we have to lean one way or another — we can't sit on the fence that marks off both realities, the rational and the mystical worlds of our experience. But both remain present. If we opt for belief in angels, we are still nagged by the skeptical rationalism of the day that pervades our common culture. But if we opt for scientific, rational empiricism, we still have this sense that some transcendent meaning eludes our grasp. As Taylor says, "People go on feeling a sense of unease at the world of unbelief: some sense that something big, something important has been left out, some level of profound desire has been ignored, some greater reality outside us has been closed off."[11]

Taylor writes that we all, more or less, live on this cultural cusp, swayed by both rational and religious impulses. We make our way in our individualistic society as isolates, uncommitted to traditional communities of synagogue or church, groping our own way toward some larger meaning, embracing some kind of fragile faith in the process.

Of course, Taylor also recognizes the counterforces of zealous enclaves and countercultural movements. For example, the Amish resist military service as pacifists and publicly opt out of the American way to follow their tradition's ways. But although some of these movements clamor loudly to be heard in public debate, these are beleaguered mi-

10. Berger, *A Rumor of Angels,* p. 95.
11. Charles Taylor, *Varieties of Religion Today* (Cambridge: Harvard University Press, 2002), p. 56.

norities in an essentially secular society. Religion in America today is mainly a do-it-yourself, individualistic creation, founded on subjective intuition (those rumors of angels), only loosely connected to a larger community of believers.

The title of Taylor's book, *Varieties of Religion Today,* echoes William James's classic, *Varieties of Religious Experience.* And we began our discussion of imagination and faith with James's elegant analysis of the subjective experience of God or an intuitive sense of transcendent Presence. Although written a century ago, James's book remains provocatively relevant today because of his focus on the individual's experience of God or Holy (Wholly) Other, those glimpsed "signals of transcendence" that Berger spoke of in our own day. James's description of religious experience resonates with our contemporary sense of "something more," even within the fleeting experience of the skeptics among us. This gut-level intuition of God's hovering presence is key to James's abiding genius and his popular relevance for contemporary, lone travelers on the road to create some overall meaning for their lives.

Of course, the self's struggle to create and express a sense of whole, authentic life is not new in our day and wasn't new even in James's day; it extends back to Coleridge and the romantic period of subjective self-expression and the creation of meaning through poetry and art. But what is new, as Taylor points out, is that now this self-expressiveness is a "mass phenomenon." And as David Brooks describes it, it has become the American way of life.

Taylor concludes that "many people are not satisfied with a momentary sense of wow! They want to take it further, and they're looking for ways of doing so."[12] The ways of doing so include many of the individual and communal practices I've described in the last two chapters of this book, practices aimed at exercising and strengthening the imagination, which lies at the heart of faith.

Although it is critical to recognize the character of our selves as fundamentally individualistic — selves striving for authentic, personal meaning within a competitive, market-driven system of rewards and punishments — the fact also remains that many find their way into religious communities of their choice, not necessarily of their family heritage. This includes both the "seekers," who are trying as individuals to

---

12. Taylor, *Varieties of Religion Today,* p. 116.

cobble together some kind of coherent religious life for themselves, moving in and out of communities as these meet their spiritual needs of the moment, and the "dwellers," who identify with a particular worship community over a longer period of time. Moving beyond the intuitive, "wow" moment of meeting Transcendence, many people affiliate themselves with other like-minded souls to assist their own piecing together of a meaningful life story. And since "God made man because he loves stories,"[13] this is where we will now turn at the end of our journey together.

Weaving Together a Good Life Story: Imagining Your Life

Someone has said that the human brain is designed for storytelling, and now there is even a whole area of neuroscience devoted to studying the neural circuitry of the narrative mind. Our dreams at night might be bizarre, but they still have a first-this, then-that sequence to them, as our brain pieces together some kind of weird story. From the beginning of our time together in this book, I have spoken of our minds' inherent capacity to think in terms of stories, to shape imaginatively our experience — our memories and our hopes — into narratives that give purpose to our lives.

Dan McAdams has spent his career interviewing adults at midlife and analyzing their life stories. He sees these stories as acts of imagination that weave together our past memories, our current lives, and our expected personal futures. My story tells you who I am, how I got here, and where I see my life going. Life stories are personal myths that you and I begin to create in adolescence and early adulthood in order to give our lives purpose and unity, to create a core identity and an overall meaning for our lives. And the making of our stories is not finally over until our lives have ended. Through a dynamic process of growth and change, we continue to write and rewrite our narratives all the way through to the last chapter.

McAdams asks this interesting question: "What do you know when

13. Elie Wiesel, quoted in Dan McAdams's *The Stories We Live By* (New York: Guilford Press, 1993). For some of my ideas in the following section, I wish to give credit to this work by McAdams, as well as his later book, *The Redemptive Self* (New York: Oxford University Press, 2006).

you know a person?"[14] There are many ways of answering this question. For example, you can focus on a person's inborn traits (e.g., you can see Suzy as a shy introvert) or analyze personality styles and behavioral adaptations (e.g., you can see Frank as an extroverted blowhard, a glad-hander and jokester in a crowd). But the deepest level of knowing someone, the most comprehensive and intimate level of knowing, is to know how they see and tell their life story. It's at the level of life story that your own lived experience meets the cultural context that feeds your imagination and shapes your narrative. And it is this personal narrative that finally gives some overall significance to your life.

At the cultural level, David Brooks describes the character of the American myth or "sacred story" that most of us take up and make our own to varying degrees. And McAdams expands in an elegant way this common story that fuels our imagination as Americans. Think Horatio Alger, and you'll have the basics of the story — Horatio Alger persevering through hardship and winning the prize.

But of course, there are variations on this theme. There are as many personal stories as there are persons to tell them, and as there are cultural symbols and myths to feed each person's narrative. McAdams says that self and culture come to terms with each other through narrative, and that our imagination lies at the base of it all:

> Culture . . . provides each person with an extensive menu of stories about how to live, and each of us chooses from the menu. Because different people within a given culture have different experiences and opportunities, no two people get exactly the same menu. We cannot eat everything off the menu we do get, so our narrative choices spell out, more than anything else, our precise relationship with our culture. . . . *We choose and we appropriate in the making of a narrative identity. We select from competing stories, and we modify those stories we choose to fit our own unique life,* guided by the unique circumstances . . . by our family backgrounds and educational experiences; and by the . . . traits and characteristic adaptations that also comprise our individuality. *A person constructs a narrative identity by appropriating stories from culture.*[15]

14. Dan McAdams, *The Redemptive Self* (New York: Oxford University Press, 2006), p. 280.

15. McAdams, *The Redemptive Self,* p. 289; emphasis added.

American culture, which of course includes religious subcultures within its mix,[16] offers a variety of stories, of plots and elements and building blocks for our imaginations to seize and feed into our story-making minds in order to create meaning and purpose and a personal sense of it all.

Everyone carries around a "Big Picture" and some sense of where their own personal story fits into the larger scheme of things. (I discussed this at length in Chapter Three.) Some stories are better than others, serving to make an integrated whole of a life well-lived. Some stories express hope and trust in a benign Transcendence whose purpose draws us forward. Some stories give blessings in the telling.

By contrast, other stories are tragic, limited, flattened, stagnant, and negative. But stories that are limited or "just no good" — as McAdams puts it — can be rewritten. Once they are told and thus experienced as a narrative whole, they can be rewritten and transformed within a communal context that provides symbols of life, not death, a context that offers a "menu of stories" about how to live a grace-filled life in the process.

In the midst of a demythologized, secular world, you and I can search out the narrative material for our imaginations in order to weave them into good stories that we can offer to ourselves, to our children, and to our friends. As McAdams says, the stories we live by are created, not found.[17] And it is in the imaginative making of them that our lives come to have their deepest meaning.

The Good Story: Four Criteria

Throughout the pages of this book, I have described our imaginative meeting of Transcendence — in direct, mystical-like encounters,

---

16. Most, if not all, religious subcultures within the United States — except perhaps some outliers and countercultural denominations such as the Amish — reflect a certain American ethos in their expression. Even Roman Catholicism and Orthodox Judaism frequently express an independence from their worldwide counterparts. Some local Catholic hierarchies have sometimes run afoul of curial pronouncements, prizing individual conscience and reason over authoritative dictates. Mission activities reflect a typically American "can do" mentality in tackling the world's troubles.

17. McAdams, *The Stories We Live By*, p. 274.

through ritual and music, visual art and poetry, and through the stories and grand myths of our culture. We meet Transcendence through all these imaginative products rooted in our cultural context. Even the most abstract creations of expressionistic art nevertheless draw on materials and forms derived from cultural stores. Despite our American individualism, we nevertheless dwell in a social context, a community of other individuals who share the same cultural terrain and its artifacts with us.

We are communal beings, we humans. And ritual, art, and story are meant to be shared. Artistic works mean little or nothing unless we engage them in a kind of dialogue; we read novels with both the characters and the author; we share both sacred and profane stories with one another as we share the stories of our lives — if only we can find a sympathetic ear to listen.

Across this book's chapters, then, we have returned to the dynamic process of conversation, of hospitality and openness to art and to the other, to engagement with cultural artifacts that can feed our souls as vehicles of Transcendence. And so I want to turn in this last section of the book to conversation and to the creation of a good life story. In the process, I will draw on our discussion of the imagination and its essential role in the development of religious belief.

There is something powerful in telling your story to another. I say this as a psychologist and former therapist, and I say this as a pastor. But I also say it as a human being, as one who has friends and who has listened to other stories and told my own story over coffee or lunch. In the previous chapter I spoke of having a soul friend, of finding someone sympathetic who can listen to your story and who can look with you for gleamings of God in your daily imaginative experience.[18] Again, some stories are better than others. Some stories are life-affirming, filled with hope. Some personal life stories create a meaningful whole, conveying a sense of God's *shalom* and the promise of redemption, a deep sense of hope-filled purpose and a trust that in the end, all will be well. Other stories fall short of this. They are fragmented, foreshortened, flat, pessi-

18. Dan McAdams has developed an elaborate and detailed conversational outline to follow in uncovering and understanding your life story in the company of a companion willing to listen to and explore your imagined "Big Picture" with you. See Chapter 10, "Exploring Your Myth," in *The Stories We Live By*.

mistic or even nihilistic — or at the very least, cynical in tone and out-look. But as I said earlier, the poor story can still be transformed, even in later life. But you cannot transform the story of your life unless you understand the one you currently imagine.

What is a good life story? Or, to be more specific, what is a good life story given the assumptions laid out here from the outset? What makes a good life story given that God exists, that God impinges on your story-telling and my storytelling, on our imaginative capacity, allowing us to meet God in a dynamic process of meaning-making over time?

In the Coda at the end of Section I, I laid out some truth criteria against which we can test the validity of our imaginings — in this case, the goodness of our life stories, which give us some sense of wholeness and integrity, of meaning and purpose in our lives. I think most of these are directly applicable to this final discussion. A good life story, as I see it, is situated within the cultural and theological context of Judeo-Christianity, and the truth criteria described in the Coda reflect that fact. But again, I believe this discussion applies to other faith traditions as well.

The *first* truth criterion addressed in the Coda is historical criteria. There are certain core, decisive events for believers that no amount of imaginative spinning can eliminate, without doing central violence to the whole traditional belief system. But for Christians, in addition to the historical figure of Jesus and the central place of the resurrection story, and in concert with other monotheistic religions, there emerges across the whole of Judeo-Christian Scripture a sense of hope, a tenor of ultimate trust in God's goodness and the final redemption of human-kind in the end.

Thus, if in telling your life story what unfolds is a sense of hope for redemption in the end and a basic trust in a benign Other who wills you well, then your Big Picture (thus far) can be considered good. If your story expresses a sense of despair, of hopelessness, of nihilistic "no exit" — then transformation is called for.

The *second* criterion for our imagined world of meaning is based on empirical and moral criteria for truth. Human reason has contributed to moral and theological development over our cultural history, and our Western civilization has come to appreciate the equal value of all human beings, irrespective of race, gender, sexual orientation, or age. The generation of an imaginative worldview or personal story that projects otherwise — for the self or for others — would be considered false and in need of transformation. A personal story that affirms such moral values for yourself and others in your own community is, according to this criterion at least, a good one.

The *third* truth criterion has to do with continuity of tradition, or continuity between your grasp of meaning expressed in your personal story linked with a single, historical tradition's wisdom. An example may help here. Suppose you were raised in one of the monotheistic traditions and thus were grounded in a world of meaning shaped by the symbols and stories of Christianity, Judaism, or Islam. But in addition, based on some aspect of Hindu tradition, your expectation for future life comes to include an imagined reincarnation, and so the next time around you might return as an eagle or a goddess or some such. And suppose you also borrow a little from the Wiccan literature, with a little Zen ideal of nonself thrown in to complete your own individual, symbolic world of meaning. Clearly, there is simply no continuity here between your "Big Picture" story constructed piecemeal from several different traditions and the communally shared wisdom of that root, monotheistic tradition.

From the vantage point of this particular book — that grounding of the imagination in a tradition's communally shared wisdom gives some overall coherence to your world's meaning — your story would not be such a good one, and transformation might be desirable. In general, then, the test for this third truth criterion of a good life story would call for engagement with a monotheistic religious tradition, using its symbols, art, and sacred stories to weave a worldview, a personal story embedded in the tradition's context of belief.

The *fourth* and final truth criterion by which to judge the goodness of your created life story, and at the center of this book, is the criterion of imaginative engagement. Of course, all of these criteria have the imagination's power at their core. But this specific one has to do with openness to engagement with the culture's aesthetic works, which enliven and color the imagination's rich projections. McAdams cites such "openness" to experience as part of a vital (as opposed to a stagnant) life story. The artistic expressions that would feed into the kind of story we've considered here include rituals, liturgy, poems, visual art, music, and fictional stories, both sacred and secular, which provide patterned visions of how a good life might proceed, become better, become enriched along the way toward some final wholeness.

A good life story would then reflect a vital and open engagement, a hospitable engagement with the tradition's aesthetic products informing the self's horizon of meaning and feeding the life story. Therefore, if a life story is stagnant — flattened, disenchanted, and empty of culture's rich symbols and metaphors as vehicles of Transcendence and hope, reflecting instead "no exit" and despair — then the life story is not good in this sense and is in need of vital transformation.

If your life story that unfolds in the telling is woven together with images drawn from, for example, such literary works as Eliot's *Little Gidding* and Shakespeare's *King Lear* and Arthur Miller's *The Crucible* and even Job's cry of lament, but you envision final hope in the face of God's whirlwind, then your story reflects depth and richness at its core. If your story is inspired by imaginings drawn from symbolically rich music such as Verde's *Requiem,* and from paintings such as Picasso's *Guernica* and Grünewald's *Crucifixion,* and from films like Scorsese's *Last Temptation of Christ* — then, according to this fourth criterion, your story is, in all likelihood, good and expresses levels of meaning that might well sustain you to the end.

A Final Word

George Steiner observes that no matter how dormant our imaginations might be, we all have known gifts of Presence, unexpected entrances of Presence into our lives. He tells of browsing in a bookstall in a Frankfurt train station and leafing through a thin book of poems by a then-unknown artist by the name of Paul Celan. Steiner skimmed through the pages and apparently was arrested by the poet's language, with phrases such as "north of the future" having a stunning effect on him at that time. Even so brief an encounter with Celan's poetic artwork seemed to open up the sense of transcendent Presence for Steiner, who reports that "Paul Celan has never left me."[19]

These poet's words became grafted onto Steiner's soul, and such engaged reception of the aesthetic opened up a space of recognition, of engagement with truth at some core level, of a sense that "we have met

19. George Steiner, *Real Presences* (Chicago: University of Chicago Press, 1989), p. 180.

before."[20] And such moments of epiphany are grace-full meetings with Transcendence, flooding our consciousness with meaning and opening out onto new horizons, new depths of understanding in the process.

Such engagement with culture's aesthetic artifacts is not just a matter of exposure but a receptive opening up, as we would open up to a guest, providing hospitality, opening ourselves to discovery, trusting the possibility of some deep truth emerging from the encounter. Based on trust that something true can be said, that there is some possible correspondence between images, symbols, and words spoken and the truth of the matter before us, Steiner argues for an ethic of reception, requiring openness to a possible truth being conveyed.

Although I believe all this is true, I must offer a final caveat. Steiner recognizes — and we have recognized all along — that messages are being created and sent by the writer and artist. These messages can be good or evil, and thus the imaginative product can enhance or diminish the humanity of both individuals and the community.

Thus, as creators of images and as consumers of the imagination's artifacts, you and I have a responsibility to choose carefully what culture has to offer. As responsible creators — in both what we imagine and what we make of others' imaginings — we must (I feel strongly enough about this to use "must"), in looking for signals of Transcendence, choose carefully at least the subculture we embrace. We must select responsibly the context we surround ourselves with — the art we engage, the movies we see and the novels we read, the music we listen to — and most especially and most crucially, choose very, very carefully our conversation partners, our soul friends along the way.

The God-given power at the core of being human, that power of the imagination to create new meaning through aesthetic engagement, makes us "close neighbours to the transcendent," Steiner says. "Poetry, art, music are the medium of that neighborhood." Steiner quotes Sir Thomas Browne: "We know that we are men and we know not how; there is something in us that can be without us, nor cannot tell how it entered into us."[21] The artist, the poet, the fiction writer, the musician — all create epiphanies where God shines through, and in our imagination's response to such openings, we meet the Divine.

20. Steiner, *Real Presences,* p. 180.
21. Steiner, *Real Presences,* p. 215.

Finally, let's end where we began — with the metaphor of our life's Saturday. All of us, every one of us, knows the Good Friday of pain and loss, of paradoxical limits to our human condition, of mortality and the unknown mystery beyond death. And all of us — believers, unbelievers, and those in between — know something about the longing for Sunday, the longing for *shalom* and wholeness and resurrection, for redemption, hoping in some sure justice and love that will conquer death in the end.

But in the meantime, "ours is the long day's journey of the Saturday,"[22] the long day's journey into that good night. Between the tragedy, suffering, brutality, and evil of today and the hope of resurrection, between the dark death of Friday and the promise of wholeness and redemption of God's Sunday, we have each other, and we have our human capacity to imagine meaning beyond the terror and the darkness. We all have the power to choose life and not death, to survive our Saturday lives and to imagine some story of Sunday wholeness that will sustain us to that end. By the grace of God, so shall it be.

22. Steiner, *Real Presences*, p. 232.

Practical Resources

Below are selected works — some already listed in the body of this book, and some additional resources — that I particularly recommend for further reading. I also recommend the quarterly journal *Image* (www.imagejournal.org), which publishes original fiction and poetry as well as interviews, essays, and articles focusing on the visual arts.

General Resources

Avram, Wes. *Where the Light Shines Through: Discerning God in Everyday Life.* Grand Rapids: Brazos Press, 2005.

Bass, Dorothy C. *Practicing Our Faith: A Way of Life for a Searching People.* San Francisco: Jossey-Bass, 1997.

———. *Receiving the Day: Christian Practices for Opening the Gift of Time.* San Francisco: Jossey-Bass, 2000.

Bond, Fiona. *The Arts in Your Church.* Carlisle, U.K.: Piquant Press, 2001.

Cox, Harvey. *Common Prayers: Faith, Family, and a Christian's Journey through the Jewish Year.* New York: Houghton Mifflin, 2001.

Csikszentmihalyi, Mihaly. *Creativity.* New York: HarperCollins, 1997.

De Waal, Esther. *Lost in Wonder: Rediscovering the Spiritual Art of Attentiveness.* Collegeville, Minn.: Liturgical Press, 2003.

Johnson, Paul. *Creators.* New York: HarperCollins, 2006.

Mariani, Paul. *God and the Imagination.* Athens: University of Georgia Press, 2002.

Martin, James, S.J. *My Life with the Saints.* Chicago: Loyola Press, 2006.

McAdams, Dan P. *The Stories We Live By: Personal Myths and the Making of the Self.* New York: Guilford Press, 1993.

Teresa of Ávila. *The Interior Castle.* Edited and translated by E. Allison Peers. New York: Doubleday/Image, 1989.

Ritual Practices

Anderson, Herbert, and Edward Foley. *Mighty Stories, Dangerous Rituals.* San Francisco: Jossey-Bass, 1998.

Biziou, Barbara. *The Joys of Everyday Ritual.* New York: St. Martin's Press, 1999.

Henke, Linda Witte. *Marking Time: Christian Rituals for All Our Days.* Harrisburg, Pa.: Morehouse Publishing, 2001.

Klein, Patricia. *Worship without Words.* Brewster, Mass.: Paraclete Press, 2000.

Prayer Practices

Bloom, Anthony. *Beginning to Pray.* New York: Paulist Press, 1970.

Brother Lawrence of the Resurrection. *The Practice of the Presence of God.* Translated by Donald Attwater. Springfield, Ill.: Templegate, 1974.

Cairnes, Scott. *Love's Immensity: Mystics on the Endless Life.* Brewster, Mass.: Paraclete Press, 2007.

Flemings, David. *Modern Spiritual Exercises.* New York: Image Books, 1983.

Johnston, William. *Christian Zen: A Way of Meditation.* New York: Harper & Row, 1979.

Keating, Thomas, and M. Basil Pennington. *Centering Prayer in Daily Life and Ministry.* New York: Continuum, 1998.

————. *The Diversity of Centering Prayer.* New York: Continuum, 1999.

Pokrovsky, Gleb, trans. *The Way of a Pilgrim: The Jesus Prayer Journey.* Woodstock, Vt.: Skylight Paths Publishing, 2001.

Silf, Margaret. *Companions of Christ: Ignatian Spirituality for Everyday Living.* Grand Rapids: William B. Eerdmans, 2004.

Williams, Rowan. *The Dwelling of the Light: Praying with Icons.* Grand Rapids: William B. Eerdmans, 2003.

Prose and Poetry

Buechner, Frederick. *Godric.* San Francisco: HarperSanFrancisco, 1980.

————. *Speak What We Feel (Not What We Ought to Say): Reflections on Literature and Faith*. San Francisco: HarperSanFrancisco, 2001.

Carlson, Paula J., and Peter S. Hawkins. *Listening for God: Contemporary Literature and the Life of Faith*. 2 vols. Minneapolis: Augsburg Fortress, 1994, 1996.

Ferlo, Roger. *Sensing God: Reading Scripture with All Our Senses*. Cambridge, Mass.: Cowley Publications, 2002.

Jackson, H. J., ed. *Samuel Taylor Coleridge: Selected Poetry*. New York: Oxford University Press, 1994.

Malone, Nancy M. *Walking a Literary Labyrinth: A Spirituality of Reading*. New York: Riverhead Books, 2003.

McEntyre, Marilyn Chandler. *The Color of Light: Poems on Van Gogh's Late Paintings*. Grand Rapids: William B. Eerdmans, 2007.

Nichols, Bridget. *Literature in Christian Perspective: Becoming Faithful Readers*. London: Darton, Longman & Todd, 2000.

Peacock, Molly. *How to Read a Poem . . . and Start a Poetry Circle*. Toronto: McClelland & Stewart, 1999.

Zaleski, Carol, and Philip Zaleski. *The Book of Heaven: An Anthology of Writings from Ancient to Modern Times*. Oxford: Oxford University Press, 2000.

Visual Art and Film

Baugh, Lloyd. *Imaging the Divine: Jesus and Christ-Figures in Film*. Franklin, Wis.: Sheed & Ward, 2000.

Calderhead, Christopher. *One Hundred Miracles*. New York: Welcome Books, 2004.

Johnston, Robert K. *Reel Spirituality: Theology and Film in Dialogue*. Grand Rapids: Baker Academic, 2000.

Children's Resources

Bell, Martin. *The Way of the Wolf: The Gospel in New Images*. New York: Phoenix Press, 1970.

Berryman, Jerome. *Godly Play: A Way of Religious Education*. San Francisco: HarperSanFrancisco, 1991.

Goldstein, Jeffrey, ed. *Toys, Play, and Child Development*. New York: Cambridge University Press, 1995.

Liao, Jimmy. *The Sound of Colors: A Journey of the Imagination.* New York: Little, Brown, 2006.

Sasso, Sandy. *God's Paintbrush.* Woodstock, Vt.: Jewish Lights Publishing, 1992.

Wuthnow, Robert. *Growing Up Religious: Christians and Jews and Their Journeys of Faith.* Boston: Beacon Press, 1999.

Yust, Karen. *Real Kids, Real Faith: Practices for Nurturing Children's Spiritual Lives.* San Francisco: Jossey-Bass, 2004.

Pastoral Resources

Davis, Ellen F. *Imagination Shaped: Old Testament Preaching in the Anglican Tradition.* Valley Forge, Pa.: Trinity Press International, 1995.

Harris, Maria. *Teaching and Religious Imagination: An Essay in the Theology of Teaching.* San Francisco: HarperSanFrancisco, 1987.

McGrath, Alister C. *Incarnation.* Truth and the Christian Imagination Series. Minneapolis: Augsburg Fortress Press, 2005.

———. *Redemption.* Truth and the Christian Imagination Series. Minneapolis: Augsburg Fortress Press, 2006.

———. *Resurrection.* Truth and the Christian Imagination Series. Minneapolis: Augsburg Fortress Press, 2008.

Wilson, Paul Scott. *Imagination of the Heart: New Understandings in Preaching.* Nashville: Abingdon Press, 1988.

Bibliography

Alston, William P. *Perceiving God.* Ithaca, N.Y.: Cornell University Press, 1991.

Alter, Robert. *The Art of Biblical Narrative.* New York: Basic Books, 1981.

Anderson, Herbert, and Edward Foley. *Mighty Stories, Dangerous Rituals.* San Francisco: Jossey-Bass, 1998.

Auden, W. H. *Collected Longer Poems.* New York: Random House, 2002.

Barth, J. Robert. *Romanticism and Transcendence.* Columbia: University of Missouri Press, 2003.

———. *The Symbolic Imagination.* New York: Fordham University Press, 2001.

Baumgaertner, Jill Pelaez. "Hints of Redemption." *Christian Century,* 21 February 2006, pp. 38-41.

Bausch, William. *Storytelling: Imagination and Faith.* Mystic, Conn.: Twenty-Third Publications, 1995.

Beer, John, ed. *S. T. Coleridge: Poems.* Everyman's Library edition. New York: Alfred A. Knopf, 1991.

Begbie, Jeremy. *Theology, Music, and Time.* New York: Cambridge University Press, 2000.

———, ed. *Beholding the Glory: Incarnation through the Arts.* Grand Rapids: Baker Academic, 2001.

Bell, John. "Sing a New Song." *Christian Century,* 25 July 2006, pp. 20-23.

Bell, Martin. *The Way of the Wolf.* New York: Walker & Company, 1984.

Berger, Peter. *A Rumor of Angels.* Garden City, N.Y.: Doubleday/Anchor Books, 1969.

Berger, Peter, and Thomas Luckmann. *The Social Construction of Reality.* Garden City, N.Y.: Anchor Books, 1967.

Berry, Wendell. *Given: New Poems.* Emeryville, Calif.: Shoemaker Hoard (an imprint of Avalon Publishing Group, Inc.), 2005.

Berryman, Jerome W. *The Complete Guide to Godly Play,* 3 vols. Denver, Colo.: Living the Good News, 2002.

———. *Godly Play.* San Francisco: HarperSanFrancisco, 1991.

Bond, Fiona. *The Arts in Your Church.* Carlisle, U.K.: Piquant Press, 2001.

Brooks, David. *On Paradise Drive.* New York: Simon & Schuster, 2004.

Brown, David. *Discipleship and Imagination: Christian Tradition and Truth.* New York: Oxford University Press, 2000.

———. *Tradition and Imagination.* New York: Oxford University Press, 1999.

Brueggemann, Walter. *An Introduction to the Old Testament: The Canon and Christian Imagination.* Louisville: Westminster John Knox Press, 2003.

———. *The Prophetic Imagination.* Minneapolis: Augsburg Fortress Press, 2001.

Buechner, Frederick. *Speak What We Feel.* San Francisco: HarperSanFrancisco, 2001.

Byassee, Jason. "Emerging Model." *Christian Century,* 19 September 2006, pp. 20-24.

Cairnes, Scott. *Love's Immensity: Mystics on the Endless Life.* Brewster, Mass.: Paraclete Press, 2007.

Clark, Cindy Dell. *Flights of Fancy, Leaps of Faith.* Chicago: University of Chicago Press, 1995.

Coleridge, Samuel Taylor. *Biographia Literaria, or Biographical Sketches of My Literary Life and Opinions.* Vol. 7 of *The Collected Works of Samuel Taylor Coleridge.* Ed. James Engell and W. Jackson Bate. Princeton: Princeton University Press, 1983.

———. *The Statesman's Manual,* in *Lay Sermons,* ed. R. J. White, pp. 1-114. Vol. 6 of *The Collected Works of Samuel Taylor Coleridge,* ed. Katherine Coburn. Princeton: Princeton University Press, 1972.

Coupland, Douglas. *Generation X: Tales for an Accelerated Culture.* New York: St. Martin's Press, 1991.

———. *Life after God.* New York: Simon & Schuster/Pocket Books, 1994.

Cram, Ronald. "Knowing God: Children, Play, and Paradox." *Religious Education* 91, no. 1 (1996): 55-73.

Csikszentmihalyi, Mihaly. *Creativity.* New York: HarperCollins, 1997.

Driver, Tom F. *Liberating Rites.* Boulder, Colo.: Westview Press, 1998.

Durkheim, Émile. *The Elementary Forms of Religious Life.* Trans. Karen E. Fields. New York: Free Press, 1995. Originally published as *Les Formes elementaires de la vie religieuse: Le systeme totemique en Australie.* Paris: Alcan, 1912.

Dykstra, Craig. "Youth and the Language of Faith." *Religious Education* 81 (1986): 163-84.

Edwards, Cliff. *Van Gogh and God.* Chicago: Loyola University Press, 1989.

Ehrenreich, Barbara. *Dancing in the Street.* New York: Henry Holt & Company, 2006.

Eliot, T. S. *The Use of Poetry and the Use of Criticism.* Cambridge: Harvard University Press, 1933.

Engell, James, and W. Jackson Bate, eds. *The Collected Works of Samuel Taylor Coleridge.* 16 vols. Princeton: Princeton University Press, 1983.

Fiddes, Paul, ed. *The Novel, Spirituality, and Modern Culture.* Llandybie, Great Britain: Dinefwr Press, 2000.

Fleming, David, S.J. *Modern Spiritual Exercises.* New York: Image Books, 1983.

Gallagher, Nora. *Things Seen and Unseen.* New York: Alfred A. Knopf, 1998.

Goleman, Daniel. *Emotional Intelligence: Why It Can Matter More than I.Q.* New York: Bantam Books, 1995.

Grimes, Ronald L., ed. *Readings in Ritual Studies.* Upper Saddle River, N.J.: Prentice Hall, 1996.

Harris, Maria. *Teaching and Religious Imagination.* New York: HarperCollins, 1987.

Hauerwas, Stanley, and L. Gregory Jones, eds. *Why Narrative? Readings in Narrative Theology.* Grand Rapids: William B. Eerdmans, 1989.

Hays, Richard. *The Conversion of the Imagination: Paul as Interpreter of Israel's Scripture.* Grand Rapids: William B. Eerdmans, 2005.

Hearne, Brian. "God's Story in Our Story." *African Ecclesial Review* 26 (1984): 32-46.

Hecht, Anthony. *The Hidden Law: The Poetry of W. H. Auden.* Cambridge: Harvard University Press, 1993.

Holmes, Richard. *Coleridge: Darker Reflections, 1804-1834.* New York: Pantheon Books, 1998.

————, ed. *Samuel Taylor Coleridge: Selected Poems.* New York: Penguin Books, 1994.

James, William. *Varieties of Religious Experience.* Centenary edition. New York: Routledge, 2002.

Jasper, David, and Stephen Prickett, eds. *The Bible and Literature.* Oxford: Blackwell Publishing, 1999.

Jensen, Robin. *The Substance of Things Seen.* Grand Rapids: William B. Eerdmans, 2004.

Johnson, Mark. *The Body in the Mind.* Chicago: University of Chicago Press, 1987.

Johnston, Robert. *Reel Spirituality.* Grand Rapids: Baker Academic, 2004.

Karr, Mary. *Sinners Welcome.* New York: HarperCollins, 2006.

Lakoff, George, and Mark Johnson. *Metaphors We Live By.* Chicago: University of Chicago Press, 1980.

Levertov, Denise. *Denise Levertov: Selected Poems.* Ed. Paul Lacey. New York: New Directions, 2002.

———. *New and Selected Essays.* New York: New Directions, 1992.

Malone, Nancy M. *Walking a Literary Labyrinth.* New York: Riverhead Books, 2003.

Mariani, Paul. *God and the Imagination.* Athens, Ga.: University of Georgia Press, 2002.

Marsh, Clive, and Gaye Ortiz, eds. *Explorations in Theology and Film.* Malden, Mass.: Blackwell Publishing, 2004.

Maxwell, Elizabeth, and Susan Shapiro, eds. *Food for the Soul.* New York: Church Publishing Company, 2004.

McAdams, Dan. *The Redemptive Self.* New York: Oxford University Press, 2006.

———. *The Stories We Live By.* New York: Guilford Press, 1993.

McEwan, Ian. *Saturday.* New York: Doubleday, 2005.

McFarland, Thomas. *Originality and Imagination.* Baltimore: Johns Hopkins University Press, 1985.

Miller, Arthur. *The Crucible.* New York: Bantam Books, 1968.

Nichols, Bridget. *Literature in Christian Perspective: Becoming Faithful Readers.* London: Darton, Longman & Todd, Ltd., 2000.

O'Connor, Flannery. *The Complete Stories.* New York: Noonday Press, 1972.

O'Siadhail, Michael. *Our Double Time.* Trowbridge, Wiltshire, England: Cromwell Press Ltd., 1998.

Peacock, Molly. *How to Read a Poem . . . and Start a Poetry Circle.* Toronto: McClelland & Stewart, Inc., 1999.

Price, Reynolds. *A Whole New Life.* New York: Penguin Books, 1995

Rosengren, Karl, Carl Johnson, and Paul Harris. *Imagining the Impossible.* Cambridge: Cambridge University Press, 2000.

Rosenthal, Peggy. *The Poets' Jesus.* New York: Oxford University Press, 2000.

———. *Praying the Gospels through Poetry.* Cincinnati: St. Anthony Messenger Press, 2001.

Salzman, Mark. *Lying Awake.* New York: Alfred A. Knopf, 2000.

Sasso, Sandy. *God's Paintbrush.* Woodstock, Vt.: Jewish Lights Publishing, 1992.

Schechner, Richard. *The Future of Ritual.* New York: Routledge, 1993.

Schneiders, Sandra M. *The Revelatory Text.* Collegeville, Minn.: Liturgical Press, 1999.

Scott, Nathan. *The Broken Center.* New Haven: Yale University Press, 1966.

Silf, Margaret. *Companions of Christ: Ignatian Spirituality for Everyday Living.* Grand Rapids: William B. Eerdmans, 2005.

Steiner, George. *Real Presences.* Chicago: University of Chicago Press, 1989.

Taylor, Charles. *Sources of the Self: The Making of the Modern Identity.* Cambridge: Harvard University Press, 1989.

———. *Varieties of Religion Today.* Cambridge: Harvard University Press, 2002.

Tetlow, Joseph, S.J. *Ignatius Loyola: Spiritual Exercises.* New York: Crossroad, 1992.

Thomas, R. S. *The Poems of R. S. Thomas.* Fayetteville: University of Arkansas Press, 1985.

Thurston, Bonnie. *Hints and Glimpses.* Abergavenny, Great Britain: Three Peaks Press, 2004.

Turner, Victor, and Edith Turner. *Image and Pilgrimage in Christian Culture.* New York: Columbia University Press, 1978.

Wallace, Catherine. "Faith and Fiction: Literature as Revelation." *Anglican Theological Review* 78, no. 3 (1996): 382-403.

———. "Storytelling, Doctrine, and Spiritual Formation." *Anglican Theological Review* 81, no. 1 (1999): 39-59.

Williams, Rowen. *Lost Icons: Reflections on Cultural Bereavement.* London: T&T Clark, 2003.

Willis, Paul. *Common Culture.* Boulder, Colo.: Westview Press, 1990.

Wolterstorff, Nicholas. *Art in Action: Toward a Christian Aesthetic.* Grand Rapids: William B. Eerdmans, 1980.

Wonder, Nancy. "Teaching Imagination Skills to Lower SES Delinquent Youth." *Dissertation Abstracts International,* Section B: "The Sciences and Engineering," 58 (6-B), December 1997, 3344. Ann Arbor, Mich.: University Microfilms International.

Wright, T. R. *Theology and Literature.* Oxford: Blackwell Publishing, 1988.

Wuthnow, Robert. *Growing Up Religious.* Boston: Beacon Press, 1999.

Yust, Karen-Marie. *Real Kids, Real Faith.* San Francisco: Jossey-Bass, 2004.

Index